Whittling Handbook

Whittling Handbook

Peter Benson

First published 2016 by
Guild of Master Craftsman Publications Ltd
Castle Place, 166 High Street, Lewes,
East Sussex BN7 1XU

ISBN 978-1-78494-075-1

A catalogue record for this book is available from
the British Library.

Publisher: Jonathan Bailey
Production Manager: Jim Bulley
Senior Project Editor: Wendy McAngus
Editor: Stephen Haynes
Managing Art Editor: Gilda Pacitti
Designer: Simon Goggin
Photographers: Anthony Bailey and Peter Benson

Colour origination by GMC Reprographics
Printed and bound in Turkey

Dedication
*To my good friend Rip Stangroom who sadly
passed away in 2010. Without the hospitality
of Rip and his family I would probably not have
travelled to the United States and rediscovered
the joy of knife carving.*

Contents

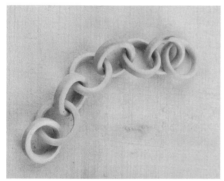

Introduction **8**
What tools will I need? **10**
How do I keep the knife sharp? **12**
What wood can I carve? **14**
How do I start? **16**
Knife choices **18**
My toolbox **20**

PROJECTS
Garden dibber **22**
Paperknife **26**
Fork **30**
Kitchen spatula **34**
Whistle **38**
Butter spreader **42**
Spoon **46**
Fox **50**
Chorister **56**
Cane topper **62**
Backscratcher **66**
Shelf Santa **72**
Door wedge **78**
Dog-head stick handle **82**
Nuthatch **90**
Perching bird **96**
Geehaw whimmy diddle **102**
Chain **106**
Love spoon **112**
Higgledy-piggledy houses **118**

Suppliers **126**
About the author **127**
Acknowledgements **127**
Index **128**

Introduction

To whittle is 'to trim, carve, slice off pieces of wood with a knife', or 'to reduce the amount of something by repeated subtraction'. So says the Oxford English Dictionary. Carvers, however, have made their own interpretations in different times and places.

One school of thought restricts whittling to working solely with a knife, usually some kind of folding pocketknife, with no other tools or surface treatment being allowed. In the UK, whittling can refer to any kind of small carving generally held in the hand. In this book we will cover working in general with green (undried) wood or offcuts of dried timber, using a variety of knives and other tools.

WHY CARVE WITH A KNIFE?
The big advantage of this hobby is that there is no great initial expense. You can get under way with just a sharp knife, a safety glove, perhaps an apron, and a piece of wood. Even the wood can be found in the garden or countryside for no cost at all. If you want to go further it might be useful to add a couple of small gouges but, really, not much else is necessary that cannot be found in the average home workshop or shed. Many experienced carvers with a toolbox full of carving tools still love the versatility of carving with a knife. It can be done anywhere and there is no bulky equipment to carry.

Although carving with a knife is widespread in the USA, with classes available in nearly every state, it has yet to become widely popular in the UK, where knife carving has always been associated with small boys working with a penknife and a stick. With today's over-protective attitudes, of course, it is very rare for a child to have any sort of

experience with sharp tools. I think, also, that many purists in the art world see anything different from the traditional methods of architectural carving or sculpture as being without any real merit.

In general, anything that can be held in the hand can be carved with a knife – any difficulties experienced will be as a result of using wood that is too hard for your hand strength or a knife that is not sharp enough, or of trying to cut off too much wood in one go.

Don't be too fussy about your first knife. As long as it can be sharpened to a keen edge, it will be adequate. You will find out fairly quickly if it is ideal for you, or whether you need to get something different. A good knife should be comfortable in your hand and not give you blisters or a sore hand. I started as a small boy with a simple small penknife or pocketknife, and regularly had to stop for a while to allow my hands to heal. Nowadays there is no shortage of choice should you want to get something different. If you wish to carry the knife with you, choose a folding pocketknife, but if you intend to work only at home you may prefer a locking or fixed-blade knife (see the legal implications on page 18).

Have a look at the carvings that we are going to try in this book, and pick out the ones that appeal to you – many have variations. They are arranged in what I consider to be an increasing order of difficulty, so I am sure you will find one to get started on.

Good luck!

Peter

What tools will I need?

NOW THAT YOU HAVE DECIDED TO GIVE KNIFE
CARVING A TRY, YOU WILL NEED TO START GETTING
THE NECESSARY EQUIPMENT. LUCKILY, THERE IS NOT
MUCH THAT YOU NEED.

YOUR KNIFE

Typical pocketknives similar to the
ones pictured (see right) will do to begin
with. If you don't have anything suitable
and wish to purchase a knife, you will
find some further suggestions on pages
18-19. You might want to add a supply
of plasters (adhesive bandages) since, no
matter how careful you are, you will get
the occasional nick, sometimes from just
picking up your knife. Safety and care
should always be at the top of your list.

*A simple penknife may be all you
need to get started. A knife with
a fixed or lockable blade is safer to
use, but may not lawfully be carried
in some places.*

YOUR GLOVE

Anyone, no matter how experienced,
should always wear a safety glove when
carving with a knife. Good, effective
safety gloves can be found online or
from specialist suppliers, including
those listed on page 126. However,
only those gloves with the appropriate
safety certification are suitable.

In the UK, for example, gloves have
to conform to the British Standard BS EN
388 and are classified according to four
criteria: abrasion (1-4), cut (1-5), tear
(1-4) and puncture (1-4). The higher the
number, the better the protection. You
should be concerned particularly with cut
and puncture, where you need as near

SAFETY TIP

Don't try to catch your knife if you
drop it. Let it fall to the ground and
then pick it up. It is easier to fix
a knife than a cut hand or leg.

...ety glove with a high rating ... cut and puncture protection is an essential piece of whittling equipment. The scores for the different protection criteria can be seen below the shield symbol.

...good
...clearly.
...nerally
...or Dyneema®
...; all are very
...the Dyneema more
co... ...sier for holding the
work... ...ot like working with a
glove, but ... un assure you that, even with
the greatest care, accidents can happen
and, with any knife, the results can be
extremely painful and even disastrous.
In my classes I will not let anyone carve
with a knife without wearing a glove.

One final word on this subject, after
I have probably frightened you all, is that
protective equipment is never foolproof
and should not take the place of safe
working practices.

YOUR APRON

If you like to carve holding the wood
in your lap, a leather apron will give
you some protection against stray
cuts, dropped tools or random knife
movements in delicate areas of your
anatomy. I discovered this early in my
carving career and was very lucky that I
didn't do any permanent damage.

SAFETY TIP

Before buying a safety glove, check
that it conforms to the relevant
safety standards in force in your
country or state.

How do I keep the knife sharp?

A SATISFACTORY KNIFE CUT SHOULD BE CLEAN AND SHINY, AND A LONG SHAVING SHOULD BE FORMED WHEN CUTTING ACROSS THE GRAIN. IF THIS IS DIFFICULT TO ACHIEVE OR TOO MUCH EFFORT IS NEEDED, THEN YOUR KNIFE IS PROBABLY NOT SHARP.

You can use any sort of flat abrasive to get an even bevel on each face of the blade. An oilstone, wet and dry paper on a flat surface (such as glass), or a diamond sharpening plate will all do this quite satisfactorily.

Preliminary sharpening on a diamond plate. An oilstone can be equally effective.

Some knives have a flat bevel over the whole of each face of the blade, while others have a slight convex curve. If the bevel is flat, you will need to keep the blade flat on the abrasive at all times. If it is curved, you need to lift the back of the blade a little from the stone. What is really important is that the area immediately behind the cutting edge should always be kept flat. This coarse sharpening process will only need doing occasionally if you look after your knife. It produces a ragged edge or 'burr' that will need honing to a fine edge before you can start carving.

Final honing on the strop.

The fine honing process, which needs to be done about every 30 minutes or so of carving time, involves polishing the knife on both sides until all sign of the burr is removed. This is done on a strop, generally made from a piece of leather glued to a wooden backing board, but canvas webbing can be equally effective.

The strop is dressed with an abrasive paste; I use the sort of chrome cleaner you can get in a tube from shops selling car-care products. Make sure that you sharpen at least two thirds of the blade from the tip. The third nearest the handle is often blunted to avoid injury to the holding hand.

The blade needs to be honed in exactly the same position as before, either flat on the surface of the strop or with the back slightly raised as appropriate. Wipe the blade along the surface away from you, with the back of the blade leading (so you cannot cut into the strop), and exerting a little pressure as you go. When you get to the end of the strop, turn the blade over and wipe it back towards you. The first time you do this, it will probably take about ten or twelve passes each way before the knife will cut cleanly. Any subsequent stropping should only need about six passes. Don't be tempted to flap your knife backwards and forwards in a mistaken imitation of Sweeney Todd the demon barber, or you will end up rounding off the edge and you will need to start the whole process over again. Your knife should now be ready to use.

Strops made from leather (top) and webbing (below), with simple home-made backing boards.

SAFETY TIP

If you are using a folding knife, be extremely careful while sharpening and honing to prevent your knife blade from folding back into the handle. A knife with a locking blade will remove all possibility of the blade folding and causing injury.

What wood can I carve?

THERE IS NO RULE THAT DICTATES WHAT WOOD YOU CAN OR CAN'T USE WHEN WHITTLING. BASICALLY, ANYTHING THAT YOU CAN HOLD IN YOUR HAND AND CUT WITH YOUR KNIFE IS SUITABLE.

Some woods are obviously harder than others, and you should try whatever you can get hold of and see if you can carve it comfortably. Avoid those that are difficult for you. Wood hardens as it dries out, so 'green' wood, freshly cut from woods or hedgerows, is softer than timber that has been commercially cut and kiln-dried.

FOOD SAFETY

If you are going to use your carving in contact with food, some woods are not suitable. Avoid exotic woods like the mahoganies and rosewoods (*Swietenia, Khaya, Dalbergia* spp.) and most of the shrubs like laburnum (*Laburnum anagyroides*), rhododendron (*Rhododendron* spp.) and yew (*Taxus* spp.), as some of these are toxic.

You should be quite safe (unless you are actually allergic) using any of the fruitwoods, such as apple (*Malus sylvestris*), pear (*Pyrus communis*), plum (*Prunus domestica*), orange or lemon (*Citrus* spp.) etc., as well as most of the temperate hardwoods. Birch (*Betula* spp.), lime (linden) or basswood (*Tilia* spp.), the maples (*Acer* spp.; these include European sycamore) and hazel (*Corylus* spp.) are

safe as long as there is no spalting. This can be recognised by black or coloured patterns appearing in the wood as a result of a fungal infection, and infected timber can be harmful, particularly when sanded.

In general I would advise that you carve woods that you recognize rather than random pieces of doubtful origin that you have picked up in the countryside.

SAFETY TIP

It is wise to take precautions when sanding any wood, particularly if using power or if the wood is very dry. A basic disposable face mask costs next to nothing. Protective eyewear is recommended when using a drill.

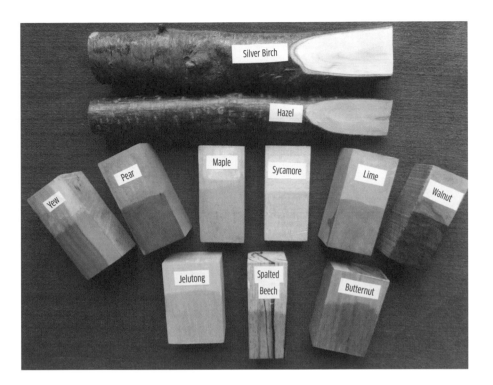

WHERE CAN I GET SUITABLE WOODS?

Ready-prepared carving wood can usually be sourced only from specialist suppliers. Lime (or basswood in North America) and jelutong are good choices to start with, as they can be fairly easy to carve.

If you intend to start with found or green wood, this will need to be cut during the winter months, as it will bleed sap if cut during the growing season. Local tree surgeons may have a wealth of green timber that they don't want. If you have suitable trees in your garden it might be worthwhile cutting timber and storing it until you want it. This can be done by wrapping suitably sized pieces in kitchen paper and storing them in a cool place – perhaps even a freezer, if you are sure this will not cause domestic strife.

If you wish to forage in the countryside you must get the permission of the landowner. Generally you can pick up wood from the floor, but don't bother with anything that is dead or diseased. Not only is dead wood very hard, but it can also be extremely brittle and may contain harmful bacteria or fungi.

Most of the projects in this book have been carved in apple, silver birch or hazel for the cut sticks or lime, jelutong, butternut or walnut for the kiln-dried woods.

How do I start?

HERE ARE FOUR BASIC CUTS THAT YOU WILL NEED TO MASTER. PRACTISE EACH CUT ON A SMALL PIECE OF STICK. YOU WILL FIND SOME EASIER THAN OTHERS, BUT PERSEVERE, FOR THEY ALL HAVE THEIR USES.

I apologize to the left-handers out there, but for ease of description I have referred to the hand holding the knife as the right hand and the one holding the wood as the left.

1 The wedge cut is made with the edge of the blade, not the point. This is a downward cut, but may involve adding a slicing motion away from you. Don't slice towards yourself, as the point of the knife can come out of the cut and cause injury. Cut into the wood at an angle, then make another cut in the opposite direction, creating a wedge-shaped groove. This groove is called a stop cut, because you can cut into the groove from either direction without slipping and causing damage. Your right thumb should remain in contact with the wood at all times.

SAFETY TIP

Be careful when you get to the end of a push cut, unless working towards a stop cut, as you can lose control of the blade as it comes out of the wood – which makes this cut inadvisable in a class or group environment.

2 In the pull or squeeze cut you pull the blade towards you by squeezing the knife towards your thumb. Try to keep your right thumb on or behind the wood, away from the path of the knife.

3 The push cut entails simply pushing the blade with the cutting hand, with or without the help of the left thumb. This is best done into a stop cut.

SAFETY TIP

Use a thumb guard or protective tape on your right thumb to avoid minor cuts or nicks. Masking tape or cohesive bandage (available from pet shops or pharmacies under many different names) are most suitable. Or you could wear safety gloves on both hands, or a leather thumb guard.

4 The lever cut is done by keeping the left thumb in contact with the base of the back of the blade and pulling the handle towards you with the right-hand fingers, using the thumb as a fulcrum to create a long slicing action as the blade moves forwards. This is the easiest action to use, with practice, and can remove large amounts of wood fast.

With all these cuts it is better, wherever possible, to keep the right hand in contact with your body and let the hand holding the wood do most of the moving. This prevents the knife from going wild – that is, waving around in the air – and reduces significantly the likelihood of cutting yourself. Don't get despondent if you have problems at first: practice makes perfect.

Knife choices

YOU CAN USE ANY KNIFE THAT YOU HAVE TO CARVE
MOST KINDS OF WOOD THAT YOU MAY WISH TO USE.
THE ONLY CRITERION IS THAT THE STEEL MUST BE
OF A SUFFICIENTLY HIGH STANDARD TO BE ABLE TO
MAINTAIN A SHARP EDGE FOR A SUSTAINED PERIOD.

If you are likely to be carving in your home or workshop, you might be better off with a fixed-blade or locking knife. These are safer as they can be used more freely and have no likelihood of folding when honing on a leather strop. Also, fixed-blade knives tend to be more comfortable or, if not, they can be made to be so.

In the UK, however, there are legal problems if you wish to carry a knife in public. A folding knife with a blade under 3in (7.5cm) in length is perfectly legal, but any sort of fixed or locking knife may not be carried 'without good reason'. If knives are in a toolbox with other carving material, one would hope this would be all right, but a knife left in your pocket or car could be an embarrassment. Be warned!

Many different knives or blades can be obtained by mail order or online from carving supplies companies such as those listed on page 126. There is not space to describe them all here, but it's easy enough to compare catalogues and see what appeals to you. Don't go out and spend a lot of money on a knife without trying it in your hand. If you are not able to shop in person, buy a budget knife first; once you have used it for a while, you will be able to judge how it can be improved on.

Whether you use a blade with a straight edge or a curved one is your choice, but I suggest you start with a straight-edged blade. These are safer, in my opinion, and easier to sharpen. Buy knives of different shapes as and when you need that particular design – not just because someone says they are good.

SAFETY TIP

The longer the knife blade the easier it will be to remove waste, but it will be more dangerous to use as the tip of the blade is further away from your knife hand.

MAKING A CUSTOM HANDLE

One alternative is to buy a blade only and make a handle that you can shape to suit yourself. The pictures below show how this can be done.

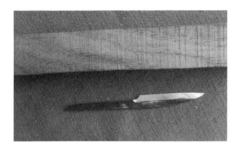

1 First choose your blade and a suitable blank for the handle. This blade is by the Welsh carving-tool specialist Nic Westermann. The handle is best made from a dense, well-seasoned hardwood such as yew, walnut or any of the fruitwoods.

2 Bore a hole into the endgrain of the handle blank that is a reasonably tight fit for the tang of the blade (if you don't have a drill press, a hand drill is quite adequate).

3 Protect yourself by wrapping the blade in masking tape before fitting it into the blank. Some blades are provided with rivet holes, but otherwise you can use two-part epoxy to hold it in place. If the blade is not quite straight in the handle, you can make allowance for this in the shaping of the handle. Shape the wood with a knife, spokeshave or rasp.

4 Handles in different shapes and materials make it easier to identify the best tool for a particular job.

My toolbox

THE PHOTOS BELOW SHOW THE TOOLS I HAVE USED TO PRODUCE THE CARVINGS IN THIS BOOK. THIS DOESN'T MEAN THAT YOU CANNOT BE SUCCESSFUL WITHOUT THIS SELECTION; YOU MAY WISH TO USE DIFFERENT ONES TO PRODUCE THE SAME RESULTS. YOU WILL ALSO NEED A STROP, MARKING EQUIPMENT, A DRILL, SUPERGLUE AND FINISHING OIL.

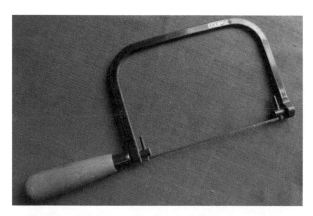

The simplest saw for cutting out shapes is the coping saw. If you have power saws that do the same job, by all means use them.

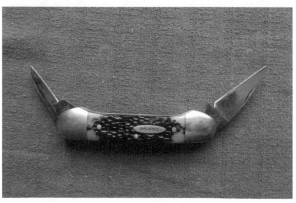

For roughing out and much of the work on the simpler projects I have used a folding pocketknife. This is easy to use, convenient to carry around and legal to have with you if out in public (see page 18). It can, however, be uncomfortable to work with for very long periods.

For fine detail and getting into difficult areas I use a detail knife with a small, fixed blade.

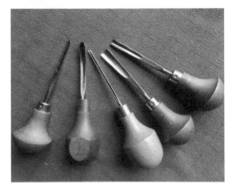

Sometimes it is convenient to use a small gouge. These come with either a fine pencil-grip handle or a small, bulbous one (the latter are often called palm gouges). Most good carving-tool manufacturers have a range of these.

Abrasives can be of many different styles but I prefer to use a cellular variety, which is not only very flexible but retains its abrasive quality without clogging. Any dust can be shaken or tapped out easily, making it very economical to use.

Garden dibber

THIS IS ONE OF THOSE IMPLEMENTS THAT YOU WILL
HAVE DONE WITHOUT FOR YEARS BUT, ONCE YOU
HAVE ONE, YOU WONDER HOW YOU USED TO MANAGE.
IT IS INVALUABLE FOR TRANSPLANTING SMALL OR
LARGE PLANTS, MAKING TRENCHES IN SEED TRAYS
FOR SOWING SEEDS, OR NUMEROUS OTHER MINOR
JOBS THAT INVOLVE SEEDLINGS AND PLANTS.

The pattern is relatively unimportant – it just needs to
make small holes in potting or garden compost. You can
decorate it in any way you like, and it would make sense
to include graduated marks along its length to give an
idea of the correct depth for each seedling. While you
can use a piece of a small branch of any size up to about
1½in (40mm) in diameter, ideally you will need a piece
about 1in (25mm) in diameter and 6–8in (150–200mm)
long. I have used a piece of green, or undried, apple from
the garden, but you could use any wood available.

TOOLBOX
- Knife and strop
- Safety glove
- Finishing oil

Variations

Below left Two tent pegs and a plant
label done in apple.
Below right Two plant labels carved
from dry hazel sticks.

1 Mark a line around the stick about 1in (25mm) from one end and another about ⅛in (3mm) from the first.

2 Using a wedge cut from each line, remove the wood between them to a depth of about ¼in (6mm), creating a V-shaped stop cut around the stick.

3 With the stop cut in place you can start removing the bark from the longer part of the stick.

TIP

The larger the pieces you are trying to cut off, the harder work it will be. Relax and take your time – you will feel better for it in the morning!

4 Use a push cut to remove the bark, cutting towards your stop cut.

5 Using a long push cut, remove the bark from the other end of the stick.

6 Continue with push cuts to shape the end of the stick to a point. Don't make it too sharp; the end can be rounded off.

7 Round off the top end of the stick with further push cuts, and remove the bark if you wish.

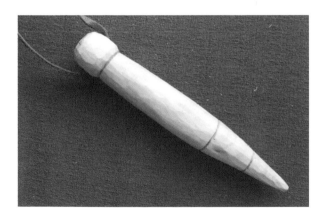

TIP

If you have carved your piece in green or undried wood, wrap it in kitchen paper and leave it to dry out for a few days before giving it a coat of oil. This can be any wood-finishing oil that you have to hand or, if you haven't any, you can use cooking or olive oil.

8 I have cut depth rings at 1in (25mm) intervals and drilled the end to take a leather strip as a hanger. With a coat of oil your dibber is finished.

Paperknife

THIS PROJECT CAN BE DONE IN ALMOST ANY WOOD YOU MAY HAVE AVAILABLE – GREEN STICK OR WORKSHOP OFFCUT – AND IS VERY GOOD PRACTICE FOR YOUR KNIFE-CARVING SKILLS. THE BASIC SHAPE WILL TO SOME EXTENT BE DICTATED BY THE SIZE AND SHAPE OF THE PIECE OF WOOD YOU START WITH.

TOOLBOX
• Knife and strop
• Safety glove
• Abrasive
• Finishing oil

If you are using a small branch, check first whether there is any pith showing down the centre; this can cause a problem if it appears at the edge or end of the blade. I used a piece of hazel for my knife and didn't notice any pith when I started, but it did appear when finishing the blade and I had to modify the shape. Don't be afraid to change the design if problems occur – this will improve your carving.

1 Mark a band about ⅛in (3mm) wide, about 3in (75mm) from the end of the stick, to separate the handle from the blade.

2 Using a wedge cut, remove the wood inside this band to a depth of around ⅛in (3mm). This will form a stop cut for when you carve the blade.

3 Remove the bark from one side of the long end of the stick, then flatten that side of the stick from the stop cut to the end, to a depth of around 1/16in (2mm).

4 Once you have a good flat surface, repeat the process for the other side. Adjust each surface until you have around ³⁄₁₆in (5mm) thickness to make the blade.

5 Cut the bark off the edges, leaving the edge flat. Mark a straight centreline along each side and each edge to ensure that the blade will be straight. If there is any evidence of pith in the centre of your stick, adjust the line of the blade to avoid this if you can.

6 Taper the wood down to these lines. Don't leave it too thin at this stage – you should still be able to see the centreline along the edge.

TIP

Allow the design to develop as you carve, going with the way the wood reacts as you cut – don't fight it.

7 You are aiming for a diamond section at this stage, with the high point down the centre of each face of the blade.

8 Draw your preferred blade shape on one side.

9 Cut out the shape you have drawn, then redraw the centrelines down each edge.

10 If you have not managed to avoid the pith, reshape the end of the blade so that the pith is not at the cutting edge.

11 Sand all the facets of the blade so they are absolutely flat. You need to go through the grades of abrasive, using progressively finer grits, until you have removed all scratches.

12 Decorate the handle as you wish and then give the whole carving a coat of finishing oil. Olive oil is perfectly good for this, but it just takes a little longer to dry than proprietary oils.

Fork

ONE OF THE NICE THINGS ABOUT WHITTLING IS THAT YOU CAN EASILY CARVE SOMETHING USEFUL FROM A PIECE OF FOUND WOOD. IF YOU ARE CAMPING OR HAVING A BARBECUE IN THE WOODS, FORKS OF VARIOUS SHAPES AND SIZES ARE INVALUABLE AND CAN BE QUICKLY MADE FROM A SUITABLE BRANCH.

Alternatively, if the outdoors is not your thing, a selection of handmade forks can provide a talking point at any family gathering. This project is to produce a small two-pronged fork out of a hazel branch, from which you can progress to all sorts of alternative designs for whatever function you wish.

TOOLBOX
- Marker pen
- Knife and strop
- Safety glove
- Drill and ⅛in (3mm) brad-point bit
- Small palm gouge (optional), e.g. ⅛in (3mm) no. 9, or narrow-bladed knife
- Abrasive
- Olive oil for finishing

1 You will need a stick about 8in (200mm) long and 1in (25mm) in diameter. Flatten about two thirds of the length to a depth of around ⅛in (3mm), leaving the end for now as something to hold.

2 Turn the stick over and cut a slope at the end, on the opposite side to the area you have flattened. This is to make the tines of the fork.

3 On the flattened side, form a concave curve to meet the slope you have just carved (see next step picture for the intended result).

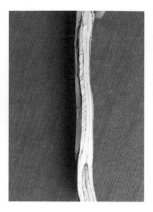

4 Square off each side of the stick to give you a flat surface to draw on.

5 Once both sides are flat, draw the shape you want the fork to be when viewed from the side. Try to match this up on both sides, but if it's not exact you can adjust this later.

6 Cut the side-elevation profile to the shape you have drawn, removing all the material you had left for holding, and then draw the pattern you want for the plan view.

7 Draw a centreline to help you check that the shape is symmetrical before removing any waste wood.

8 Cut to the lines you have drawn, keeping the edges square. If you are unhappy about the pull cut shown here, you can use a leather thumb guard or protective tape on your right thumb (see Safety Tip, page 17). Check for symmetry on both top and bottom.

9 Rest the fork on waste wood and drill holes between the tines, using a brad-pointed bit to avoid slipping. Use a drill smaller than the space, drilling slowly to avoid splitting.

10 Very carefully remove the waste between the tines with your knife. Using a pull cut, with your thumb supporting the outside of the tine, you shouldn't have a problem with the wood breaking. Keep your thumb out of the direct line of your knife blade, and use a thumb protector if you prefer. Alternatively, use a small gouge for this job.

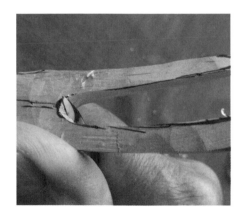

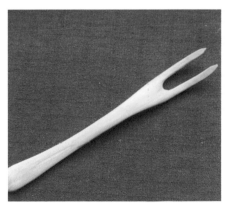

11 Your fork is now shaped and can be cleaned up and smoothed off ready for use. If you have a knife with a thin, narrow blade, this will make the whole process easier.

12 Sand thoroughly, using progressively finer grades of abrasive, until there are no rough areas. Give the fork several coats of olive oil, rubbing in well with your fingers until a satin finish is obtained. Allow to dry.

Kitchen spatula

THOUGH I HAVE USED AN OFFCUT OF WOOD FROM THE WORKSHOP, YOU CAN MAKE THIS QUITE SUCCESSFULLY FROM GREEN TIMBER AS LONG AS YOU HAVE THE MEANS TO SPLIT LARGER LOGS INTO THIN PIECES. THIS COULD BE A SPLITTING AXE OR A LARGE MACHETE-TYPE BLADE OF SOME KIND. THOSE OF YOU WHO POSSESS A BANDSAW SHOULD BE ABLE TO CUT SUITABLE SLICES VERY EASILY.

The pattern shown is the same as one that we have been using at home for some years, and is made from an offcut of lime (linden). European sycamore, maple, birch, basswood or fruitwood would all be equally suitable. Don't be too restricted by the shape shown – try your own variations.

TOOLBOX
- Marker pen
- Coping saw, if available, to cut outline
- Knife and strop
- Safety glove
- Small, shallow palm gouge, e.g. ⅜in (10mm) no. 3 or 4
- Abrasives
- Olive oil for finishing

Variations
Below You can make the shape of the spatula anything you wish, as long as it does the job. A few alternatives are shown here – some well used.

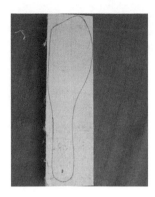  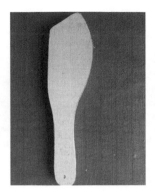

1 Prepare the timber to approximately 10in (250mm) x 2¾in (70mm) x ⅝in (15mm). Draw the outline on one side. Apart from a straight edge at the end, the shape can be anything you like.

2 Cut out the shape you have drawn with a coping saw or bandsaw. If you have neither you can use your knife.

3 Check the shape to see if it works for you before going any further.

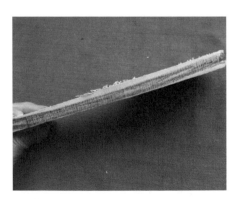 

4 You might like to put in a slight curve along the length of the spatula. This not only looks elegant, but also helps to keep the cook's fingers away from anything hot.

5 Shape the body so that it is comfortable in the hand, with no hard edges. Use a gouge to remove the waste on the inside of the curve; it's possible to do it with a knife, but the gouge is easier. Match the outside curve to ensure an even thickness.

6 Sand the whole thing, going through the grades of abrasive until you have a very smooth feel overall.

7 Mark the bevel at the end carefully, getting it as parallel to the edge as you can. The bevel can be on either side of the blade.

8 Cut the bevel with the knife and finish with abrasive until a good, flat and reasonably sharp edge is attained.

TIP

There are hundreds of different shapes that could be used for this project, and with a little modification the same basic design could be used to make a shoe cleaner or a garden spade scraper. All you need is a little imagination.

9 Once you are completely happy with the spatula's shape and feel, give it a final sanding with fine abrasive, leaving no rough areas where food will collect when it is used. All that is now needed is to give the whole thing a liberal coating of olive oil and rub it well in with your fingers. Leave to dry, and you are finished. You might want to give it a further coat of oil from time to time to keep it in good condition.

Whistle

IF YOU ARE A PARENT WITH SMALL CHILDREN, PROBABLY THE LAST THING YOU WANT TO HAVE AROUND IS A WHISTLE. DOGS LIKE SQUEAKY TOYS, TEENAGERS LIKE LOUD MUSIC AND SMALL CHILDREN LOVE DRUMS AND WHISTLES. HOWEVER, IF YOU ARE OUT IN THE WOODS OR COUNTRYSIDE, OR EVEN IN A BUILT-UP AREA, A LOUD WHISTLE CAN CERTAINLY ATTRACT ATTENTION IF NEEDED.

My wife and I keep a whistle attached to our keyring as a fob, so it serves two useful functions. So far we haven't felt the need to use it in an emergency, but you never know.

This project is just the basis upon which you can create as many variations as you wish. Once you have mastered getting the tone that you want, many of your family and friends will suddenly find a need to have one for themselves, particularly if you personalize it for them.

1 Find a piece of twig, preferably fruitwood, silver birch or European sycamore (or use offcuts from your workshop if you wish). This will need to be around 4–6in (100–150mm) long and ⅝–¾in (15–20mm) in diameter, though there really is no limit to the size. Cut your length of twig to the rough size you want. If it is to be a small whistle, I suggest that you leave some extra length for now in order to handle it more easily.

TOOLBOX

- Knife and strop
- Safety glove
- Short length of dowel, ¼–⅜in (6–8mm) in diameter
- Drill and bit, preferably brad-point, to match diameter of dowel
- Glue, such as PVA
- Split keyring
- Finishing oil or varnish

2 Drill a hole at one end, the same diameter as the dowel and approximately 2in (50mm) deep, keeping as near to the centre of the twig as you can. Hold the wood in a vice or clamp to avoid injury if the drill should break out of the side. If you don't have a vice, you could drill a larger hole in a bigger piece of timber to hold the twig while drilling.

3 Measure about ⅝in (15mm) from the drilled end and make a vertical cut across the side of the twig, marking the end of the mouthpiece. You can either do this with a small saw or with your knife. Now make a shallow, sloping wedge cut towards the vertical cut.

4 Deepen the notch so it just breaks into the hole you drilled. Try to keep the first cut vertical and the second at around 45 degrees, to create a wedge-shaped space.

5 Clean up the notch so that both edges are smooth and protrude a little way into the hole you drilled.

6 Cut a short length of dowel (just long enough so you can hold it securely), trim one end of it square and flatten it off a little on one side.

7 Insert the dowel into the mouthpiece until the square end is level with the vertical cut, and the flattened surface is uppermost and in line with the top of the mouthpiece. There should be a narrow space (the windway) in between the flat side of the dowel and the hole.

8 You can now try your whistle, adjusting the position of the dowel insert (the fipple) until you get the sound you want. You may have to spend a little time at this before you get it right, including further cleaning up of the exposed edges of the hole.

9 Once you are happy with the sound, glue the fipple in place with a suitable glue, such as PVA or similar. Check that the glue you use is suitable for putting in the mouth.

10 Shape the mouthpiece so that it is comfortable, ensuring that you don't break into the drilled hole. You might like to take off the bark where your mouth will go, but it is entirely up to you.

11 Don't go more than around ⅝in (15mm) from the end, or you could interfere with the voicing mouth – the area that makes the sound.

TIP

By varying the length, diameter, size and angle of the voicing mouth, the depth of the drilled hole and the shape of the fipple, you can achieve all sorts of different tones.

12 Drill the end of the whistle and trim to fit onto a keyring. You can decorate it in a wide variety of ways – carving, burning or painting – to make it individual, or just finish with a coat of olive oil or varnish.

Butter spreader

ALTHOUGH MOST HOUSEHOLDS HAVE A PRETTY WIDE
SELECTION OF KNIVES OF ALL SHAPES AND SIZES, FEW
PEOPLE ACTUALLY USE THEM TO CUT ANYTHING. THEY
ARE MORE COMMONLY USED TO PUSH AND SEPARATE
PIECES OF FOOD (WHICH COULD JUST AS EASILY
BE DONE WITH A FORK) OR TO SPREAD VARIOUS
SUBSTANCES ONTO BREAD.

With this in mind, my next project is to carve a butter
spreader that will, of course, spread just about anything
that you require. The shape can be almost anything you
wish, as long as it does the job and won't break, leaving
pieces of wood in your food. You will need to choose a
timber that is non-toxic. Lime, basswood, birch, sycamore
or any of the fruitwoods would be quite adequate, unless
anyone in your family is actually allergic to them. I have
used a small piece of silver birch, as it carves well and
has a very attractive grain and colour when finished. The
design is very simple and can be modified as you wish.

TOOLBOX
- Knife and strop
- Safety glove
- Marker pen
- Coping saw if you
  have one
- Abrasive
- Olive oil for finishing

1 This is a piece of silver
birch cut during the winter.
Don't cut when the tree is
coming into leaf, or it will
bleed sap profusely. I used
a short branch about 1½in
(40mm) in diameter and
6in (150mm) long.

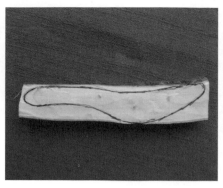

2 Flatten both sides of the stick, either by splitting off the waste or by paring it flat with a knife. Birch is much easier to cut than fruitwoods.

3 Mark out the shape you want on one side.

TIP

When removing large quantities of wood, try to let the grain of the wood help. By putting the blade into the endgrain you can induce the wood to split, which saves a lot of effort.

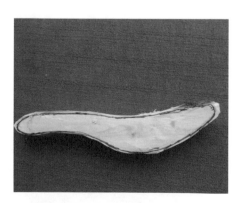

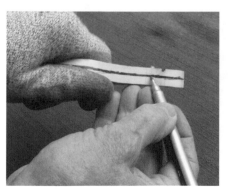

4 Cut out the shape you want, using your knife (as here) or a coping saw.

5 Draw a straight centreline along the edge of the cut-out block to ensure that the finished knife will be straight.

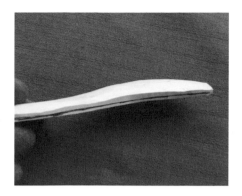

6 Thin down the whole piece to around ⅜in (10mm), ensuring that the centreline remains central, and round off the corners.

7 Pare down each side of the blade with your knife until it is reasonably smooth. Don't make the edge too thin, or it will break away – remember, it doesn't need to be sharp enough to cut with.

SAFETY TIP

Put your knife down if you want to talk to someone.

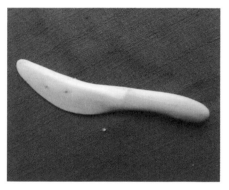

8 Shape the handle, rounding the edges so that it is comfortable in the hand.

9 Sand the surface until there are no rough areas, and make sure the blade is very smooth. Continue sanding through the grades of abrasive from around 150 to 600 grit, until there is no evidence of scratches. Once you are satisfied with the finish, give the whole thing a few coats of olive oil and rub well in with your fingers. It is now ready and safe to use with food.

Spoon

WOODEN SPOONS ARE FOUND IN ALMOST EVERY KITCHEN. NOT ONLY CAN THEY BE USED IN COOKING AND FOOD PREPARATION BUT THEY CAN ALSO BE USED AS SUGAR, SALT OR COFFEE SPOONS – IN FACT, FROM ANY JOB THAT REQUIRES SMALL QUANTITIES OF ALMOST ANYTHING. IF YOU WISH TO TAKE YOUR WHITTLING EXPERIENCE FURTHER AND TRY CARVING WELSH LOVE SPOONS, THIS PROJECT CAN BE YOUR FIRST STEP.

This basic spoon can be used in the kitchen or at the campsite, and the skills used will apply to any other spoons that you may want to carve.

Unless you have the means to split green logs easily, I would recommend that you use any offcuts of prepared wood that you may have. I have used a piece of lime (linden), as it is suitable for using with food, but birch, sycamore, maple and the common fruitwoods are equally suitable. The piece I used was 10in (250mm) long, 2½in (60mm) wide and ¾in (20mm) thick, but you can make it any size you wish by scaling these measurements up or down.

TOOLBOX
- Knife and strop
- Safety glove
- Paper (optional)
- Marker pen
- Small palm gouge, such as a ¼ or ⅜in (6 or 7mm) no. 5
- Coping saw
- Abrasive
- Olive oil for finishing

Variations
Both bowl and handle shapes can be varied as much as you like. I have kept these examples very simple because they are intended for practical everyday use. Carving a ball on the end of the handle is a great exercise in knife control.

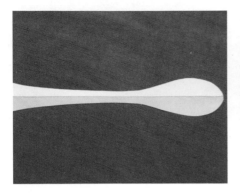 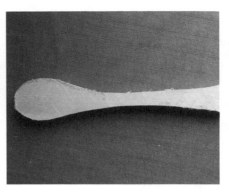

1 You might like to make a paper pattern to make sure your spoon is symmetrical. Folding the paper down the middle before cutting out will ensure perfect symmetry.

2 Draw round your pattern onto your chosen timber and cut it out with a bandsaw or a coping saw. Any slight irregularities can be sorted out as you carve.

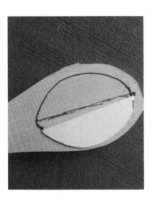  

3 Make a smaller paper pattern showing half of the hollowed-out part of the spoon and use this to draw a symmetrical outline onto your blank. If you have a really good eye then you could omit these stages.

4 Using your palm gouge, hollow out the spoon bowl, working across the grain. This will avoid overlapping shavings that tend to form in the deepest part of the bowl when cutting deep along the grain. Continue until you are happy with the shape.

5 Sand the bowl to almost a finished surface before shaping the outside; this will make the next stage easier. The scratches caused by using the abrasive in a circular motion (which is necessary to get an even surface) can be removed in the final sanding.

6 Using your knife with a mixture of push and pull cuts, shape the outside of the bowl, using your thumb and forefinger to gauge the thickness of the wall as you go along.

7 When you are satisfied that the thickness is even all over, blend in the inner shape of the bowl towards the outside edge, giving a smooth, rounded edge.

8 Finally, shape the handle as you wish, taking care to keep it symmetrical and blend it smoothly into the bowl. You may leave the handle straight or shape it in any way that pleases you.

TIP

If you have difficulty smoothing the inside, try using a scraper. If need be, you could grind an old hacksaw blade into a curve at the end and use this as a scraper.

9 Sand the spoon to a good finish, working through the grades of abrasive to get rid of any scratches. Wetting the wood before the final sanding may improve the finish. Once sanded and dry, coat with olive oil before use, rubbing it well into the wood with your fingers.

Fox

MOST PEOPLE THAT I KNOW HAVE A FAVOURITE ANIMAL, AND OF THOSE PEOPLE A GOOD PROPORTION WILL COLLECT ALL KINDS OF MODELS OR PICTURES OR ANYTHING THAT DEPICTS THEIR FAVOURITE.

This fox carving has been stylized to simplify the shape so as to make it a little easier to carve. With some modification it can be made to represent many different animals whose basic anatomy is similar.

This fox can be carved from green wood if you wish, but I have used a piece of spare wood from the workshop. I have shown a side and a front pattern for reference, and you can cut out these outlines with a coping saw or bandsaw if you have them, or cut down to the lines with your knife.

TOOLBOX
• Marker pen, card and scissors
• Knife and strop
• Safety glove
• Coping saw
• Small, deep palm gouge, no. 9 or similar (optional)
• Small, shallow gouge, no. 3 or similar (optional)
• Abrasive
• Olive oil or other finishing oil

Note: There is nothing in this project than cannot be carved with a knife, but you may find some steps easier with a gouge if you have one.

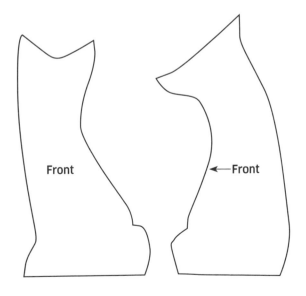

Front   ←Front

TIP

I don't recommend that you attempt carvings such as this without drawing your outlines first; otherwise you can quickly lose your way and get all your proportions wrong. Use my drawings here as a guide.

1 You will need a piece of timber 4 x 2 x 2in (100 X 50 X 50mm), and it will need to be as square as possible, with flat sides, if you are to be able to cut out the pattern easily. Trace the front and side patterns onto card. Cut these out and draw round them onto your block, making sure that you get them the right way round. You will find it easier if you draw patterns on all four faces of the block. Shade the parts to be cut away.

2 Beginning with the front elevation, remove the waste (shaded in the photo) outside your drawn lines, keeping the cut edges as square to the pattern surface as possible by matching up with the pattern you have drawn on the opposite face. This can be done with a knife or saw.

 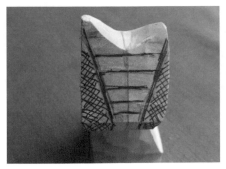

3 Cut away the waste on the side elevation and shade in any remaining waste areas. Repeat this process with all the waste until you are down to the drawn lines on all faces.

4 Draw in the centreline of the head, then add two lines as shown to mark the rough outside shape of the head. Lines drawn at right angles to the centreline will help keep the shape symmetrical.

5 Remove the waste down both sides of the head.

6 Start to round off all the corners of the body. Leave any further shaping of the head for the moment. Draw in a rough curve to represent the spine of the fox. This will change as the shape develops.

7 Round off the front corner to give a smooth curve to where the end of the tail will be.

8 Redraw the spine line down the back so that the base of the tail is at the bottom, directly below the line of the fox's left ear. Adjust the shape so this is a smooth curve.

9 Sketch in a rectangle to represent the pelvis and an area either side to mark where you need to allow wood for the haunches. Extend the line of the spine to mark the centreline of the tail. From halfway down the pelvis rectangle, sketch in the positions of the thigh bones, making sure they are of equal length.

10 Now you can shape the whole body, keeping the lines as smooth as possible. Don't put in too much detail. In this picture the knife is outlining the curve between the haunch and the body.

11 Moving to the front of the head, cut the curve in front of the ears, angling down from the centre of the head. Keep this curve as smooth as you can.

12 Two curved facets create the eye sockets and the muzzle. A drawn centreline ensures symmetry.

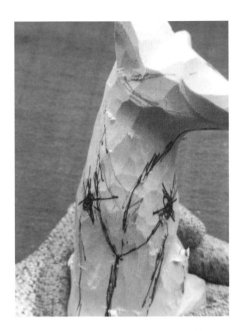

14 Shape the back of the ears and neck and blend into the body, maintaining the smooth lines.

13 Mark in the position of the shoulders and mark the centreline of the neck and chest, giving the required twist to the head. Shape this to blend in with the parts already shaped.

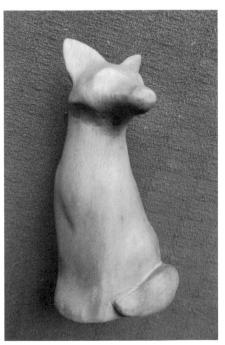

15 Sand the whole carving, going through the grits until a smooth, scratch-free finish is attained.

16 Give the whole piece a coat of finishing oil and then polish it to a satisfactory finish.

Chorister

ON ONE OF MY EARLY VISITS TO THE USA I WAS AMAZED AT HOW ENTHUSIASTIC AMERICAN PEOPLE SEEMED TO BE ABOUT THE WHOLE CHRISTMAS THING. BRITISH PEOPLE SEEM MORE CASUAL ABOUT IT, SO TO BE GREETED BY CHRISTMAS STORES AND THE HUGE RANGE OF PARAPHERNALIA AVAILABLE WAS A REAL EYE-OPENER. EVEN THE SIMPLEST OF CARVED CHRISTMAS ORNAMENTS WERE SNAPPED UP EAGERLY.

When I came home I tried out some ideas on my carving students and, to my amazement, a whole new tradition was started that has carried on for the past 20 years or so. I am now required to produce a new Christmas design each year for them to carve, and so successful have they become that carving starts earlier and earlier in order to produce enough pieces for family and friends. This project and the Santa (pages 72–7) are two of these designs that you might like to try.

TOOLBOX
- Marker pen
- Knife and strop
- Safety glove
- Small V-tool (parting tool), ⅛in (3mm) or similar
- Small, deep palm gouge (veiner), ⅛in (3mm) no. 9 or similar
- Acrylic paints and varnish

Variations
Below *You can have a lot of fun trying out different hairstyles and costume details for your celestial choir.*

1 You will need a piece of wood 6 x 1½ x 1½in (150 x 40 x 40mm). You can use green timber if you wish, but I have used a piece of jelutong from the workshop. Basswood or lime will work just as well. Mark a line about 1½in (40mm) from one end all round the block where the shoulders will be. Make a stop cut all round this line, about ⁵⁄₁₆in (8mm) deep and wide.

2 Cut off all the corners of the head block until it becomes a cylinder. Don't round it off at the top and bottom yet. Draw a centreline along each of the four faces, indicating the position of the nose and ears.

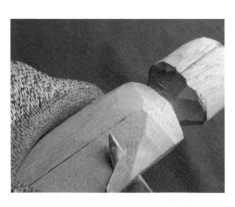

3 Round off the corners of the body on one face, sloping the shoulders into the base of the stop cut you made for the head. This will become the back of the carving.

4 Turning to the front of the carving, measure down from the stop cut about 1¼in (30mm). From either side, draw an angled line from this point upwards to the centreline, finishing just below the stop cut.

5 Cut off the waste above these marks to create the outline of the arms, the front of the shoulder and the top of the chest.

6 Form the basic collar shape below the head block, making sure to slope it downwards at the front.

TIP

Cut to drawn lines whenever you can. Don't try to cut freehand.

7 Draw a 1-1¼in (25-30mm) circle on the top of the head block. Mark at each side where wood needs to be left for the ears.

8 Cut a little outside this line for the full depth of the head, leaving some wood at the front and sides for the ears and nose.

9 Round off the head, leaving a round button for the nose and lugs for the ears. You have scope here to create your own particular character.

10 Cut along the underside of the arms, shaping the front of the body as you do so. Leave about ⅜–⅝in (10-15mm) at the elbows to give plenty of wood for the sleeves; you can always reduce this later if you wish.

11 Shape the sleeves and hands, without adding detail to the hands - keep it simple.

12 Using a small V-tool, carve in the detail of the hair. I have given this one a fringe over the eyes so that there is no need to add eyes to the face, but you can give yours whatever hairstyle you fancy.

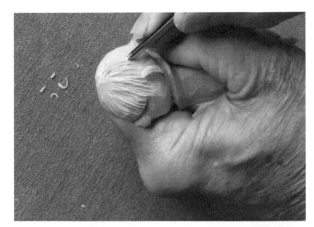

13 Now you can add the ruffles on his collar and use a small, deep gouge (a veiner) to open the mouth. Check the carving for any untidy parts, clean it up and you are done.

14 Since I use these as Christmas decorations, I paint them in acrylics with a bright finish. If you prefer just a hint of colour, dilute with about 20 parts water to 1 part paint and add coats until you get the effect you require.

Cane topper

ONE OF THE HAZARDS I HAVE ENCOUNTERED IN MY GARDEN HAS BEEN THAT OF WALKING INTO CANES THAT I HAVE PUT IN THE GROUND TO SUPPORT PLANTS AND VEGETABLES. SO FAR I HAVE AVOIDED POKING MYSELF IN THE EYE, BUT I FEEL THAT HAS BEEN MORE BY LUCK THAN JUDGEMENT.

This project aims to keep all of you that venture into the garden out of harm's way by adding something to the top of the cane to make you aware that it is there.

As with many projects in this book, I am showing one example (a pumpkin) and then suggesting what you can do with a few variations. If you like the idea then you can produce as many different designs as you wish – there really is no limit to what is possible.

There are two options here if the end product is going to be effective: the cane topper must be big enough so that you cannot possibly miss it, or brightly coloured for the same reason. Let's see what we can do.

TOOLBOX

- Marker pen
- Pencil
- Knife and strop
- Safety glove
- Coping saw if you want to remove a lot of wood
- Small, medium-sweep palm gouge, such as a no. 5 or similar
- Vice (optional)
- Drill and bit suitable for size of cane
- Paints, if required, and/or outdoor varnish or wood treatment

TIP

Don't be afraid to experiment, as these can be a great way to start designing your own individual pieces - and even the 'failures' can still be put to use in the garden.

Variations

Left It's easy to ring the changes on this project and most of the ideas shown here follow the same carving procedure.

1 You will need a piece of wood about 2in (50mm) square and 4in (100mm) long. You will use less than half of this for your project, but you will need something to hold while carving. Mark two pairs of lines all round your block, one halfway along and the other close to one end. The space between each pair of lines should be about ⅜in (10mm).

2 Using wedge cuts, make a stop cut all the way around at these two locations, to a depth of around ⅜in (10mm).

3 Reduce the wood above this second line, leaving an area around ⅜in (10mm) in diameter. This will be for the stalk of the pumpkin.

4 Now you can start to shape the pumpkin by taking off all the corners until you have a regular cylinder with a flat top and bottom. Do not try to round off in more than one plane at a time or you will end up with an irregular shape.

5 Once you are happy with the round shape, looking down from the top, you can start to shape the top and bottom. Remember that a pumpkin is not completely spherical – it is flatter top to bottom. Don't cut right through at the bottom, as you still need to be able to hold it by the spare wood.

6 Now begin to shape the stalk, taking care not to make it too thin. The top of the pumpkin will need to have a recess around the base of the stalk, and you may find it easier to use a small gouge to make this. The pumpkin stalk has a wider ring around the base, which is seen more clearly in the next photo.

8 Clean up the whole surface if needed and then, using a small, shallow gouge, lightly tool the whole surface to give a natural texture.

9 Mark the centre of the base and hold it securely, preferably in a vice, while you drill a hole through the base and into the pumpkin. Don't worry if it is not exactly central, as long as it is deep enough to fit on top of your cane. If you are worried about drilling too far, put a little flag of masking tape on the drill bit to indicate when you have reached the required depth.

7 Mark the grooves in the surface with a pencil; try to get them reasonably symmetrical but don't be too worried about this, as every one is different. Round the surface into these lines to a depth of about 1/16 in (2mm) with either a knife, V-tool or small gouge, whichever you have available. You may well use all three if you have them. Don't cut into the ring around the base of the stalk.

10 All that is now left to do is to separate the pumpkin from the spare wood, clean it up and paint it with acrylics. For outdoor use, seal it afterwards with a suitable varnish or sealer.

Backscratcher

ONE OF THE MOST FRUSTRATING PROBLEMS WE ALL FACE FROM TIME TO TIME IS WHAT TO DO WHEN WE GET AN ITCH ON OUR BACK IN A SPOT THAT IS OUT OF REACH OF EITHER HAND. NEVER FEAR, THE SOLUTION IS (SO TO SPEAK) AT HAND!

The shape of a backscratcher is not really that important; it just needs to have something protruding that can successfully find the point of irritation. I have chosen a dragon claw, but feel free to adapt the design to suit your requirements.

TOOLBOX

- Marker pen
- Knife and strop
- Safety glove
- A second knife with narrow fixed blade
- Small, deep palm gouge, e.g. ¼in (6mm) no. 9
- Abrasive
- Superglue (cyanoacrylate) or epoxy to fix claws
- Acrylic paints, varnish and brushes

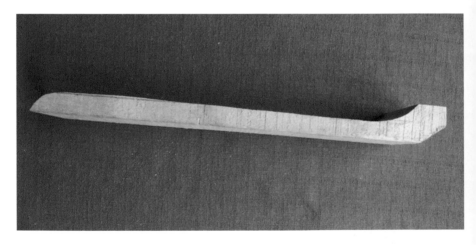

1 My design starts with a length of wood – anything you have to hand will do – about 12in (300mm) long, 2in (50mm) wide and 1½in (40mm) thick, although you can make yours longer if you wish. If you want to insert claws as I have done, you will need some short pieces of ³⁄₁₆in (5mm) dowel. Reduce the thickness of the handle by about half so as to leave a thicker area at the business end.

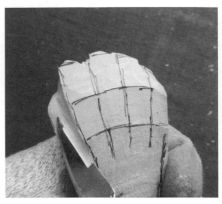

2 Taper the handle from around 2¾in (70mm) at the fat end to about 1¼in (30mm) at the narrow end. Note how easily the wood splits along the grain. You might like to sketch in the fingers to give you a guide to the shape needed.

3 Draw the rough positions of the fingers and knuckles and cut down at one side to establish the position of the thumb.

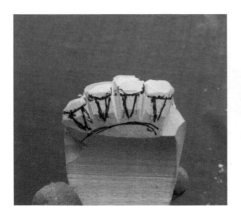

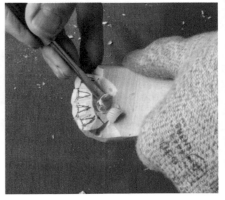

4 On the underside of the hand, sketch in the claws for reference, noting that a line drawn through all the claws should meet somewhere near the base of the hand.

5 Using your small palm gouge, hollow out the palm of the hand as far as you can for the moment.

6 Shape the backs of the fingers to match the angle of the drawn claws. If you check with your own hands you will get a good idea of the angle required.

7 Redraw the lines of the fingers and knuckles and add the plates or scales on the back of the hand.

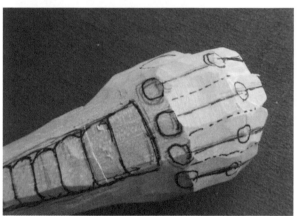

TIP

Your pencil is your most valuable tool. Draw any parts of your carving that you intend to work on. If you need to change anything, redraw it first.

8 Start to separate the fingers with your knife, taking care not to force the blade too deeply between the fingers to prevent breaking one off.

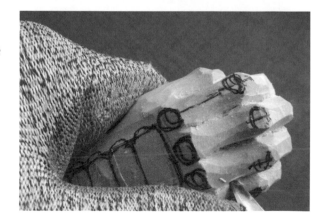

9 Continue to separate the fingers and thumb. You might find that you will be better off with a small fixed-blade knife for this.

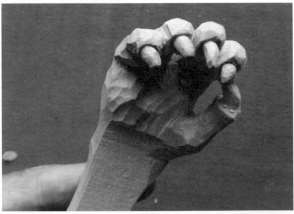

10 As the ends of the fingers are short grain and therefore likely to break in use, you can drill the ends of the fingers and insert short lengths of ³⁄₁₆in (5mm) dowel.

TIP

Another way to strengthen the claws, instead of resorting to dowels, would be to carve the claws in one piece with the hand and then soak them in superglue (cyanoacrylate) to harden them.

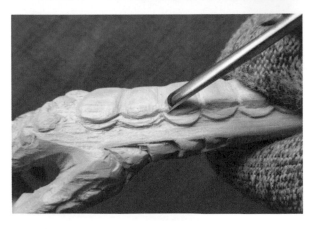

11 If you are going for the dragon look, you can now add the detail of the plates on the back. What pattern you use here is very much up to you. I have used two small palm gouges to shape these plates.

12 The knuckles are carved in a similar style.

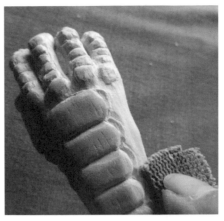

13 You will now need to clean up and sand the carving before adding a finish.

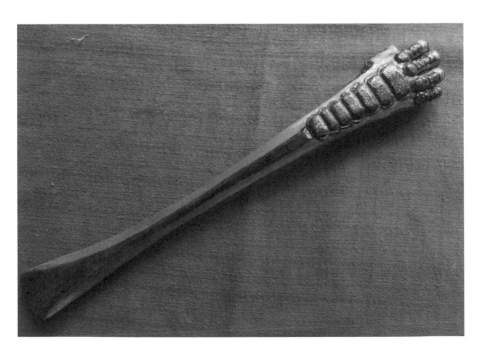

14 I felt the dragon claw would look much better if it was brightly painted, so I did this with acrylics and coated it with acrylic varnish to finish.

Shelf Santa

WE CAN CARVE FOR ACHIEVEMENT, AIMING FOR
PERFECTION AND ARTISTIC MERIT, OR WE CAN CARVE
SIMPLY FOR THE PLEASURE THAT OUR WORK GIVES TO
OTHERS. NO MATTER WHAT SORT OF WOODCARVER
YOU MIGHT BE, YOUR FRIENDS AND RELATIONS
WILL THINK YOU ARE THE BEST AND WILL LOVE
EVERYTHING YOU PRODUCE.

Even the most skilful of my fellow carvers have found
that, around Christmas time, there is a huge demand for
what I would call fun carving, and their masterpieces
have to take a back seat while they produce the carvings
hinted at by their friends and relations.

One of the most popular of these projects in recent
years has been the shelf Santa, a gnome-like figure that
can sit on any convenient shelf. You can make the figure
what you want – a traditional Father Christmas or elf,
for example – the choice is yours and any modifications
needed are slight. As for size, you can make it fit
whatever wood you have available.

TOOLBOX

- Knife and strop
- Safety glove
- Marker pen
- Narrow-bladed detail
  knife (optional but very
  useful)
- Small, deep palm gouge,
  e.g. ¼in (6mm) no. 9
- ¹⁄₁₆in (1.5mm) palm V-tool
  for the hair
- Saw to cut the angle in
  the block
- Acrylic paints, varnish
  and brushes

1 You will need a piece
of wood approximately
2in (50mm) square and
3in (75mm) long. Jelutong
is easy to carve and will
paint well. Mark an area
1¼ x 1¼in (30 x 30mm)
for the cutaway that
enables him to sit on
the shelf.

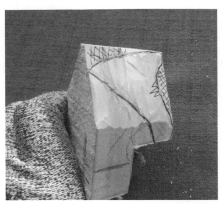

2 Cut out the marked area with either a saw or a knife, and mark out a triangle on the uncut portion to show the outline of the hat.

3 Remove the waste marked out in Step 2 and, turning to the side, mark the side view of the hat.

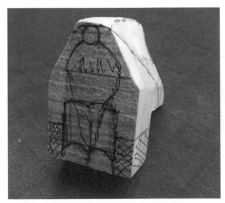

4 Cut out the shape of the hat. Keep your cuts square across the block and don't round anywhere at this stage.

5 Turn to the front of the carving and mark in the legs and any other detail you wish. The legs need to be about 1¼in (30mm) wide in total.

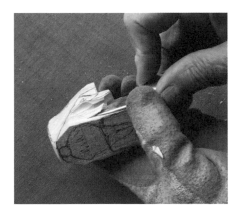

6 Cut out the shaded area all the way through to the back. Leaving about ⅜in (10mm) for the hands, continue to remove waste upwards to the hat as shown.

7 Mark an area for the feet and cut out the waste in front of the legs and beard, leaving around ⅜in (10mm) from the end of the foot to the front of the legs. Cut a small groove across the beard area to mark the top of the knees.

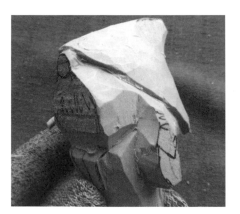

8 Cut away the waste to define the arms and outline the hat.

9 I was not happy with the shape of the hat and nose so I changed them at this stage, lowering the nose and reducing the size of the hat.

10 Now add the folds to the hat and shape the arms and body, using a knife or gouge as preferred.

11 Shape the nose and mouth to suit your chosen expression. A small gouge will be easier for the nostrils, as it will be less likely to split the wood.

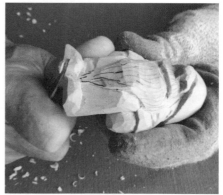

12 You can now add the creases in the sleeves and some hair poking out from under the hat. Don't try to be realistic with this, as fine detail is all too easy to break away.

13 Shape the underside of the feet and outline the beard ready for detailing.

14 Using a small V-tool, carve the hair of the beard. All cuts should be in the form of an elongated letter S, avoiding a regular pattern in order to look natural.

15 Go over the whole carving and clean up any areas that are not crisp and neat. Cut deep into the mouth to create a shadow. Your carving is now ready for painting.

TIP

Remember that the solution to all problems is to remove more wood. You just have to be sure where to remove it from!

16 For a bright finish, use the acrylics undiluted. If you prefer only a hint of colour, dilute with about 20 parts water to 1 part paint. Give the whole carving a coat of acrylic varnish or sealer, and you are finished.

Door wedge

AT SOME TIME OR OTHER I AM SURE SOME OF YOU
HAVE WALKED INTO THE EDGE OF A DOOR THAT HAS
SWUNG OPEN JUST BECAUSE IT FELT LIKE IT – I KNOW
I HAVE! THE ANSWER TO THIS PROBLEM IS VERY
SIMPLE: WEDGE IT OPEN.

We live in a thatched cottage dating back to the early
1700s and all our doors move on a regular basis.
Unfortunately the clearance under the doors is different
for every one, so different sizes of door wedge are
needed if all doors are to be covered. The measurements
shown here will need to be adjusted to suit your doors.

TOOLBOX
- Marker pen
- Knife and strop
- Safety glove
- Coping saw or similar
- ⅛in (3mm) no. 3 palm
  gouge
- ¼ or ⁵⁄₁₆in (6 or 8mm)
  no. 3 palm gouge
- Small scraper if needed
- Abrasive
- Finishing oil or sealer

TIP

If you have caught the basic form of
your subject and captured the spirit
of it, you will have little need to add
detail. It is better to undercarve
a piece than to overcarve it.

1 You can use any wood that you have available, and the
size of the wedge will depend upon the amount of space
under the door. In general I would think that you need
around 2in (50mm) depth at the thick end. Draw your
wedge shape on the wood as shown.

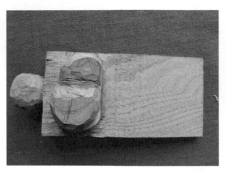

2 Cut out the basic shape with a suitable saw. A coping saw will do this quite satisfactorily.

3 I have chosen a sleeping cat for my wedge, but you can use any animal that you like. Cut the rough shape of your animal, marking the separation between head and body. At this stage you might like to give the wedge some kind of handle. I have chosen a small ball shape but you can use whatever you prefer.

4 I suggest that you set out the head first and make sure this sits correctly on the body.

5 Once you are happy with the head shape, continue with the body and tail.

6 Now give the whole carving a thorough sanding to make sure that there are no ragged edges before you add the final detail. The most difficult part is to get the top of the wedge flat. I suggest that you make it as flat as you can with a shallow gouge and then sand or scrape it to a finish.

7 Go over the whole piece and sharpen up any detail that has been smoothed out too much by the sanding, finally cleaning up ready for applying the finish.

TIP

It may seem obvious, but never scratch your nose with a knife in your hand.

8 Give your wedge a coat of finishing oil or sealer and you are done.

Dog-head stick handle

ORNAMENTAL TOPS FOR WALKING OR HIKING CANES
ARE POPULAR ITEMS AT COUNTRY OR GAME FAIRS
AND USUALLY FETCH A GOOD PRICE, EVEN IF ONLY
OF AVERAGE QUALITY. CARVERS OF HIGH-QUALITY
ONES CAN MORE OR LESS NAME THEIR OWN PRICE.

Stickmaking is a craft of its own and I will only touch
on it here, as there are many publications available that
cover the skills necessary. The dog head shown here is
that of a generic lop-eared breed and can be modified
to suit most hound-type dogs. The finished carving will
need to be fitted to a suitable straight stick, either
natural or handmade.

TOOLBOX
- Card, marker pen and scissors
- Knife and strop
- Safety glove
- Try square
- Bandsaw or coping saw
- Drill and ⁵⁄₁₆in (8mm) brad-pointed bit
- ⅛in (3mm) and ¼in (6mm) no. 9 palm gouges
- ¼in (6mm) no. 5 palm gouge
- ⅛in (3mm) V-tool
- About 4in (100mm) of ⁵⁄₁₆in (8mm) threaded studding
- Epoxy glue
- Small piece of horn (water buffalo or ram) for spacer if desired
- Abrasive
- Paint for eyes and clear nail varnish
- Finishing oil

Variations
*Here are some other examples of
heads for canes that can be carved
using similar techniques.*

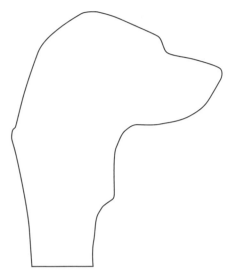

1 You will need a piece of wood 4 x 4 x 2in (100 x 100 x 50mm) thick. I used butternut. Copy or trace the pattern onto a piece of thin card and cut out to use as a template.

2 Draw the outline onto the block, making sure that the grain of the wood goes across the shank and along the line of the head (the shank will have a steel rod through the centre to give it strength). This is a general rule with carved heads, as it prevents the snout from breaking when weight is put on it.

3 Cut out the profile with a bandsaw or coping saw, keeping the edges as square as you can.

4 Drill a ⁵⁄₁₆in (8mm) hole into the centre of the bottom of the block to a depth of about 2in (50mm), or to the centre of the head. Make sure this hole is square to the bottom of the block. Ask someone to help by sighting the drill against a try square placed upright on the bench.

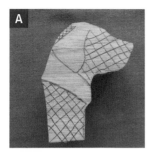

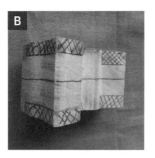

5 Draw the waste to be removed, as shown in these side (**A**) and front (**B**) views, to ensure that you have enough wood for the ears, which protrude quite a way from the head.

6 Draw in and cut the outline of the ears. Don't make them too small – you can always reduce the size later.

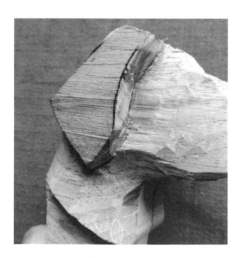

7 Narrow down the head and neck ready for shaping.

8 Round off the top of the nose and head, creating a dip in front of the eyes.

TIP

Learn as much about your subject as you can by referring to good photographs. Don't use other people's work or drawings as reference – you will only perpetuate their mistakes.

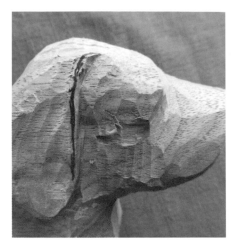

9 Start to shape the ears, leaving as much wood as possible for the fold at the top of the ear.

10 Round off the back of the head and neck, cutting in behind the ears for the back of the fold.

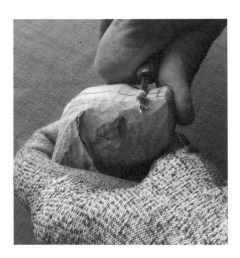

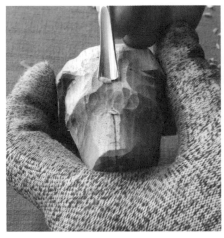

11 Now you can start to shape the bridge of the nose and the muzzle. A knife with a small, fixed blade is handy for this.

12 Using a small gouge, cut a groove down the centre of the head and blend into the bridge of the nose. This will form the brow.

13 Draw in the eye, the bulge below it and the ridge below that, which is formed by the upper jawbone. Shape these with your gouge.

14 You can now slim down the nose so that the sides are more or less parallel with each other. Check that the widest part of the head is level with the eyes, tapering towards the centre upwards and downwards. Draw in the nose and eyes.

15 Now is the time to glue the length of studding into the hole you drilled in the underside of the neck. Use two-part epoxy for this, making sure that the glue gets all the way down the hole and doesn't push the rod out as it is compressed. It may take several attempts to remove any air from the hole.

16 Thin down the front edges of the ears so that they hang vertically with a slight tip-out at the bottom.

17 You can now do the final shaping of the ears and undercut them so that they stand away from the head. The finished stick is intended to be handled, so take care not to make any part of the ears too thin, creating a risk of bits breaking off.

18 Use the no. 5 palm gouge to shape the underside of the jaw, remembering to leave a small flap at the back of the mouth where the lip hangs down (this can be seen more clearly in the next picture).

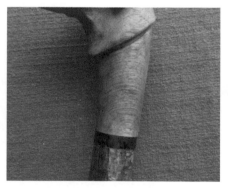

19 Before adding the final details I suggest that you fit the head to your stick. I have chosen a length of hazel, which I have straightened using a hot-air gun. Drill into the end and add a horn spacer if you wish, before gluing together with epoxy.

20 Now it is just a matter of shaping the lower part of the carving to blend in with the stick and cleaning up all over, going through the grits until a fine finish is achieved. Any blemishes will become obvious at this stage, and should be cleaned up.

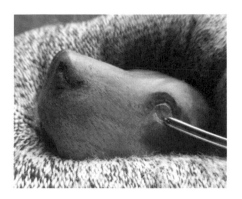

21 Shape the eye sockets, making sure that both sides are the same. When you are happy with this, cut the outline of each eye with a small V-tool and round off the edges of the eyeball.

22 If you wish to paint the eyes, do so now. To give the eyes a realistic shine, put a small drop of clear nail varnish on top of the paint when it is thoroughly dry.

23 Give the whole piece a coat of oil and you are finished.

24 This view should help to clarify the shape of the ears, and the details of the nostrils. Widening the ears would make the head look cuter, but would make it more vulnerable to damage in use.

Nuthatch

THE DETAILED CARVING OF BIRDS, ACCURATE DOWN
TO INDIVIDUAL FEATHERS, IS A VERY SPECIALIZED
ACTIVITY OUT OF THE REACH OF MOST GENERAL
CARVERS. I CERTAINLY WOULD BE EXTREMELY
RELUCTANT TO SPEND THE HOURS NEEDED FOR
RESEARCHING, CARVING AND PAINTING THIS SORT
OF WORK. THIS DOESN'T MEAN, HOWEVER, THAT WE
CANNOT CARVE BIRDS IN A SIMPLIFIED FORM.

This nuthatch is a very simplified design capturing,
I hope, the spirit of the bird yet resulting in an attractive,
tactile carving that most hobby carvers would be able to
complete to a good standard.

TOOLBOX

- Marker pen, paper or
  card and scissors
- Knife and strop
- Safety glove
- Bandsaw or coping saw
- Small no. 9 gouge or
  V-tool
- Abrasive
- Paint for the eyes (or
  pieces of water buffalo
  horn or ebony to inlay
  eyes if preferred)
- Finishing oil

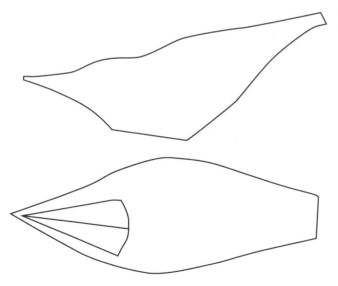

TIP

Check your proportions and dimensions
at regular intervals. Most living things
have some form of symmetry.

1 Trace or copy the top
and side patterns onto
stiff paper or thin card.
Cut out to make templates.

2 Lay out these patterns on a block of any wood of your choice (I used English walnut, as it gives a beautiful grain pattern when polished), 5½ x 2 x 2in (140 x 50 x 50mm), making sure that they line up with each other. Draw around the templates.

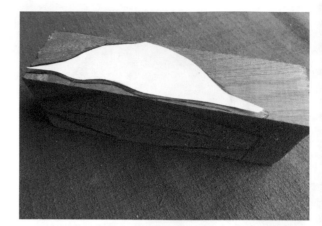

3 Cut out the shape carefully with a coping saw, or a bandsaw if you have one.

TIP

If you are in any doubt about the form of your subject, make a maquette (a small model) in clay or modelling material to get the details right.

4 Draw a triangular outline for the head and cut either side to get the shape you want. I have turned the head slightly to give it more animation, but you can keep it straight if you wish.

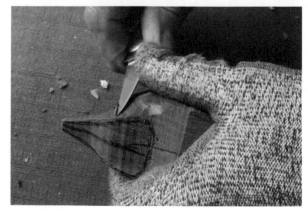

5 Roughly shape the body, making sure that you get it symmetrical around the centreline (note that the turned head has its own separate centreline).

6 Make sure the general shape of the head is right before you shape the beak. Don't make it too thin at this stage – you can always refine it later.

7 As this needs to be a smooth, tactile shape, you can now sand it to get rid of any lumps and bumps. You will probably want to make adjustments before you are happy with the shape.

8 This top view shows the turn of the head more clearly.

9 Draw a line from the tip of the beak to the back of the head, parallel with the top of the head. This is the eye line. Mark the eyes, with their centres about ½in (12mm) back from the base of the beak.

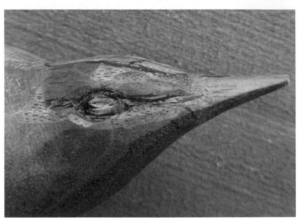

10 Draw two lines across the top of the head at right angles to the centreline, one level with the front of the eye and one with the back. This will make sure that the eyes are level. Sight from the top and front to check this before and during the carving of the eyes.

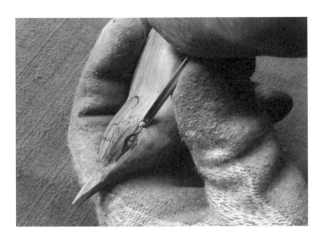

11 Use a small no. 9 gouge or V-tool to cut the groove in front of and behind the eyes, which the eyeballs will sit in.

12 Shape the eyes and their sockets with your knife or a small gouge, making sure that they are both the same. If you prefer to inlay the eyes, use the process described in the next project.

13 Now you can continue with the sanding process in order to get rid of any scratches. If you wish to fine down the beak a little more, you can do it now. If your wood is soft, I suggest that you soak the beak in superglue (cyanoacrylate) to harden it. Finally, give the whole carving a coat of finishing oil of your choice; I have used olive oil.

Perching bird

THIS PROJECT IS MERELY A BIT OF FUN. THE LITTLE BIRD, REPRESENTING A LONG-TAILED TIT THAT IS COMMON IN THE UK, IS DESIGNED TO SIT ON THE RIM OF A GLASS, MUG OR CUP. IT GOES DOWN WELL AS A PRESENT AND TALKING POINT, BUT IT SERVES NO REAL PURPOSE, UNLESS YOU WANT TO MODIFY IT TO HOLD A NAME CARD FOR A PLACE SETTING, FOR EXAMPLE.

It can be painted to represent the original bird, or used to show off a piece of wood with a particularly interesting grain pattern. In either case it is important that the finish is of a high standard and that all the lines are smooth and pleasing, so make sure that you go through the grades of abrasive to as fine a grit as you have available. I have used an offcut of butternut, but English walnut, although a bit harder to carve, gives a very pleasing effect.

TOOLBOX

- Marker pen, paper or card and scissors
- Knife and strop
- Safety glove
- Fixed-blade detail knife
- Bandsaw or coping saw
- Drill and bit, $\frac{1}{16}$–$\frac{1}{8}$in (2–3mm) diameter
- Superglue (cyanoacrylate)
- Abrasive in a range of grits, including fine
- Ebony or buffalo horn for eyes, if required
- Finishing oil

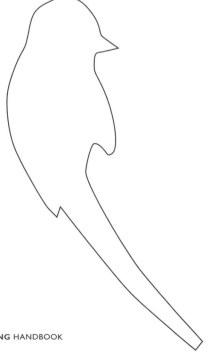

1 Trace or copy the pattern onto a piece of paper or thin card. Cut out and transfer this to a block of wood measuring 5 x 2 x 2in (130 x 50 x 50mm). Cut this out with a bandsaw if you have one, or a coping saw if that is all you have.

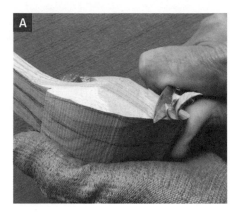
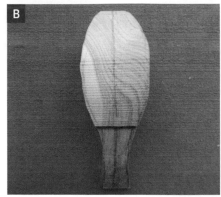

2 Using your ordinary roughing-out knife, round off the sides **(A)** until you have a pleasing shape **(B)**. This can be modified later if necessary.

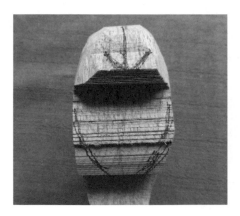

3 Mark in the beak and the curve of the body below it.

4 Form the curve of the lower part of the body and the wings at the back.

TIP

If you suspect that something is wrong but don't know what it is, turn your carving upside down or look at it in a mirror and you will almost certainly see the problem.

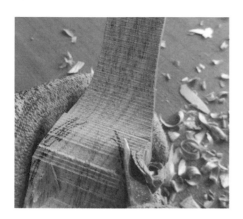

5 Start to blend these curves into the body shape.

6 Begin to shape the tail, undercutting the lower edge of the wings.

7 Use your thin-bladed detail knife to do the preliminary shaping of the beak. Draw a centreline to make sure that it is central and symmetrical.

8 Draw two lines across the centreline, one at the base of the beak and the other across the top of the head. The point where these meet should give you the location of the eyes.

9 Draw the outline of the wings, making sure the lines are the same on both sides.

10 Cut this outline with your detail knife, rotating the blade as you cut, so that you get a smooth curve between the body and the wing.

11 Moving to the front of the block, blend the body into the tail, losing all the straight edges from your original cutting out. Thin down the tail throughout its length. At this stage you need to fit the bird to the glass or cup on which you want it to balance. This will involve adjusting the groove underneath so that the bird remains stable when in place. If you have cut to the pattern it should need very little adjustment.

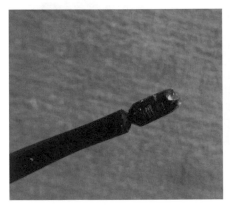

12 The next stage is optional. I have chosen to inlay the eyes with small pieces of water-buffalo horn to give them a sparkle. You could use ebony if preferred. Pare it down to make a small dowel about $\frac{1}{16}$–$\frac{1}{8}$in (2-3mm) in diameter.

13 Drill a matching hole in a piece of scrap wood to test the fit before drilling the two holes in your bird.

14 Cut partway through your dowel to make it easier to trim when fitted, then glue the end in place with superglue (cyanoacrylate) and trim off the remainder. Repeat for the other side.

15 Finally, trim the dowel back to the head with a small knife or scalpel, sand down with very fine abrasive and polish to a shine with your fingers. Give the finished bird a liberal coat of olive oil or similar, and you are finished.

Geehaw whimmy diddle

THIS TRADITIONAL AMERICAN GAME OR PUZZLE DATES BACK TO COLONIAL TIMES AND HAS A NUMBER OF SIMILAR NAMES. YOU SHOULD NOT TELL ANYONE HOW IT WORKS – THEY ARE SUPPOSED TO WORK IT OUT FOR THEMSELVES.

For the purposes of this exercise I will let you into the secret but you are honour bound not to divulge this to anyone else. You may use any instructions to make the propeller reverse, but calling 'Hooey' is the traditional way.

TOOLBOX
- Marker pen
- Knife and strop
- Safety glove
- Panel pin
- Drill and two fine bits, one a tight fit and the other a loose fit for the panel pin
- Abrasive
- Epoxy adhesive if needed
- Finishing oil

1 You will need a length of hardwood about ⅜in (10mm) square; the length doesn't really matter. Softwood won't work very well and will wear out quickly. I have used steamed pear. The second piece can be anything you have to hand and will need to be around 3½in (90mm) long, ¾in (20mm) wide and ⁵⁄₁₆in (8mm) thick. You will also need a short length of ⅛in (3mm) dowel and a long panel pin. Make sure your two pieces of wood are reasonably smooth and uniform in shape.

 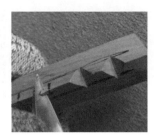 

2 On the longer piece of wood, draw two lines along its length, about ⁵⁄₃₂in (4mm) either side of one of the edges, and divide these lines into ³⁄₈in (10mm) segments.

3 Using a wedge cut, make a right-angled stop cut at each of these marks.

4 Using a fine abrasive, sand off all the sharp edges so that the stick is comfortable to hold and the high points between the notches are very slightly rounded.

5 The smaller piece of wood is to be your propeller. Mark the pivot and the boss at the centre of its length.

TIP

Since your notched stick will get a lot of wear and tear, use the hardest wood you can manage – but remember that the harder the wood, the smaller the chips you should cut.

6 Carve the angles of each blade so that one twists in the opposite direction to the other (the final shape is shown clearly in Step 9). Mark the waste carefully as shown, so you don't cut the wrong side by mistake.

7 Now drill a small hole in the centre to take the panel pin. This hole will need to be big enough to allow the propeller to rotate, but not big enough for it to slip over the head of the pin. Should you make a mistake, you can always add a drop of epoxy to the end of the pin to make it larger.

8 Using a smaller bit, drill a pilot hole in the end of the notched stick, as near to the centre as you can. Attach the propeller to the notched stick and check that it rotates freely.

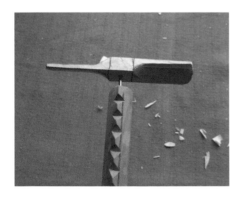

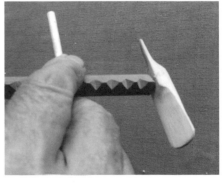

9 Before final fixing, clean the whole thing up and finish with a coat of oil. Test that the propeller rotates freely. Glue the pin holding the propeller into the end of the notched stick, if necessary, and then test.

10 When you use your dowel to rub along the notches, the propeller should rotate provided you keep your thumb in contact with one side of the stick. By removing your thumb and rubbing with your forefinger on the other side, the propeller should reverse. Traditionally you should say 'Hooey!' each time you change direction, but it works even if you don't.

Chain

**ONE OF THE GREAT FAVOURITES AMONG WHITTLING
PROJECTS IS THE CARVING OF A CHAIN. NOT ONLY
IS IT A VERY GOOD EXERCISE BUT IT HAS ALSO BEEN
WIDELY INCORPORATED INTO CARVINGS SUCH AS
LOVE SPOONS. AND EVERYONE WILL WANT TO KNOW
HOW YOU DID IT!**

The basis of all chain carving is the formation of the
cross pattern along the length of the timber. This can be
done with a straight branch by sawing away the waste
sections, but the process is considerably easier and
safer if you start with a piece of timber already square-
sectioned. With a little patience you can use a tenon
saw to cut away the four waste sections to form your
cross. For your first attempt, don't be tempted to make
the chain too long – 6in (150mm) long and 1¼in (30mm)
square is plenty big enough. Even a large V-tool could be
used to produce the shape you require, if you have one
in your toolbox. If you possess a rabbet (rebate) plane,
you may prefer to use that. Which way you choose, and
how long you spend, is very much a matter of individual
choice. Once you have this preparatory work completed
you can get on with the carving.

TOOLBOX

- Marker pen, ruler and thin card
- Knife and strop
- Safety glove
- Small gouge, ⅛ or ⁵⁄₃₂in (3 or 4mm) no. 5 or similar
- Knife with narrow, fixed blade (optional but useful)
- ⅜in (9mm) no. 39 or no. 40 V-tool (useful if using green wood)
- Drill with ⅛ or ⁵⁄₃₂in (3 or 4mm) bit
- Tenon saw
- Abrasive
- Olive oil

TIP

If you have a fixed-blade knife and
want to protect the end, use a synthetic
cork (a real cork encourages rust)
or a length of clear plastic tubing so
you can see the blade. This will also
prevent accidental cuts while in your
toolbox or roll. Never put the knife
away without its cork.

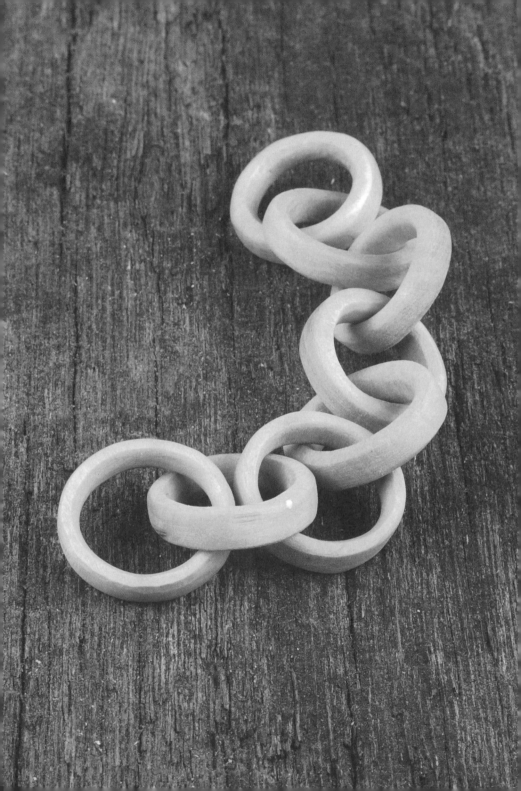

1 Divide the width and depth of the block into three equal parts and mark all round as shown. The arms of the cross will be left thick at this stage, give the wood strength as you carve.

2 Using your tenon saw, cut carefully along the length of the block, keeping to the lines you have marked. Take care not to cut too deeply. Repeat for each corner and remove the waste.

3 Here is an end view of the chain blank with the waste removed. Any irregularities in your sawing can be tidied up as you shape the links.

4 This blank is made from easily carved lime (linden). If the chain is to be part of a larger carving, the cross shape will need to be taken into account in the design.

5 Mark out the length of the links. The shape is up to you. I have made mine circular, but the longer they are, the easier they will be to separate.

6 Cut down either side of the lines you have just marked, creating a wedge-shaped stop cut. This will avoid splitting the links as you shape them. Make sure you slice away from you as you make these cuts.

7 Using a card template of the desired pattern, mark out each link on each side, making sure that the sides line up with each other.

8 Round off each link using the wedge cut, then remove the waste material that has been left at each end of the stick. Check that you have cut to the lines on both sides.

9 Once you have cut all the links to shape, mark the thickness of each link and drill several times through the waste of each one with a small drill bit.

10 Using your small gouge, carefully remove all the waste from the inside of the first link. This can be done with a small knife but is safer with the gouge, as you have less risk of splitting the wood.

11 Once you have cut out the waste from the inside, you can now cut between the inside of this link and the next, still using the small gouge. Take your time with this.

12 Using your small knife, carefully separate this first link from the next one.

13 Repeat the process for each link in turn, and trim to make all the links as uniform as possible. Keep the edges square until you are satisfied that they are flat and circular, and then you can round them off.

14 You can use abrasive to tidy up the links if you wish. I use a rolled-up net abrasive as this doesn't clog, but anything that is not too coarse will do. In this picture I have left some links unsanded for comparison.

TIP

Keep track of the grain direction as you work around the links. Remember that it will be different on the inside and outside of the link.

15 And here's how it looks when all the links are sanded. Apply olive oil with your fingers to give a finish.

Love spoon

ONE OF THE CLASSIC WHITTLING PROJECTS IS
A SMALL BALL CAPTIVE IN A WOODEN CAGE, ALL
CARVED FROM ONE PIECE OF WOOD. THERE ARE
MANY VARIATIONS ON THIS THEME, AND AS MANY
USES TO WHICH IT CAN BE PUT.

For this project I have incorporated the ball-in-cage into
a simple decorative spoon, commonly referred to as a
love spoon, which also includes a captive ring. Many of
the techniques learnt from carving the chain will help in
carving this project. Feel free to produce your own design
based on what you have learnt; don't feel that you have
to follow my instructions exactly.

TOOLBOX

- Marker pen
- Knife and strop
- Safety glove
- Pair of compasses or coin
- A small fixed-blade knife
  if you have one
- Bandsaw or coping saw
- ⅛ or ⁵⁄₃₂in (3 or 4mm)
  no. 3 palm gouge
- ⁵⁄₃₂ or ³⁄₁₆in (4 or 5mm)
  no. 5 or 6 palm gouge
- ¼in (6mm) no. 9 palm
  gouge
- Drill and ⅛ or ⁵⁄₃₂in
  (3 or 4mm) bit
- Abrasive
- Finishing oil

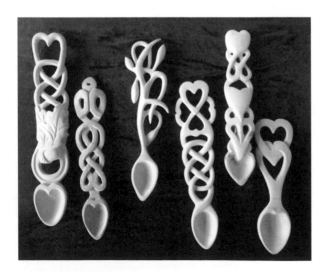

Variations

*Here are examples of alternative
spoon designs carved by Paula
Peddar, one of my students. If you
like the idea of decorative spoons but
don't want to carve the ball-in-cage,
why not try one of these?*

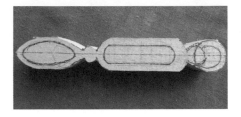

1 I have used a piece of lime, 7½ x 1¼ x 1¼in (190 x 30 x 30mm), but you can make it any size you wish and use any timber you have available. Using as hard a wood as you can carve in comfort will reduce the risk of breakage. Mark out the top profile to your desired proportions, then cut out the shape using whatever type of saw you have available. If you don't have a saw, use your knife.

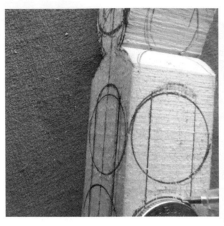

2 Using a pair of compasses or a suitably sized coin, draw the outlines of the balls, making sure that they are in the same position on each face.

3 Working from each face in turn and using a small gouge, cut out the openings above, below and between the balls, right through to the opposite side of the block.

4 You will need a narrow-bladed knife to cut the curve of each ball at the top and bottom only. Do not try to round off any more at this stage. Leave the sides connected to the side walls until you are sure you have the curvature correct at the top and bottom.

5 Mark out the side profile of the spoon and cage to your preferred pattern.

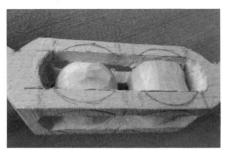

6 With a small gouge or knife you can now start to round off the sides of each ball, taking care to keep to a spherical shape. Do not rush this stage, as the quality of the finished piece will depend on how accurately the shape of the balls has been carved.

7 The curved surface of the ball should finish where you want the final thickness of the cage pillars to be, as you see with the left-hand ball here. Don't separate the balls at this stage, as they support the cage and prevent the whole carving becoming unmanageably fragile.

8 Cut the side profile to the shape you have drawn.

9 Before you thin down the top ring, drill holes through the waste material, making sure you support the spoon while you do so.

10 Cut away the waste from the inside of the ring with a small, shallow gouge to avoid cutting through the side with a knife.

TIP

If you need to rotate the knife blade to carve hollows and curves, you will be better with a narrow-bladed knife.

11 Trim the inside and outside with a narrow-bladed knife until the ring is round and of even thickness.

12 Before releasing the ring, shape the bowl of the spoon. Start with the inside, using your no. 5 or 6 gouge and working across the grain whenever possible to avoid small splits or breaking of the grain.

13 Shape the outside of the bowl, checking with your fingers to ensure even thickness all over.

 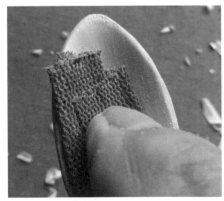

14 Form the transition between the bowl and the cage.

15 Sand the bowl of the spoon inside and out until you have a good, scratch-free finish.

16 With your small no. 3 palm gouge, gradually cut around the join between the ring and the loop at the top of the cage to separate the ring. This needs great care. I have done dozens of these successfully, but this one broke on me. Don't worry if this happens – you can insert a new piece of wood into the broken area as I did. If this part worries you, leave the ring connected to the top of the cage.

17 Clean up the ring and then sand the whole of the carving until you are satisfied with the result. This will take a while, but the amount of time you spend will be reflected in the final result.

18 You can now separate the balls from the cage by carefully cutting through the edges where the balls are fixed. Sand until round.

19 Finally, trim the inside of the cage and tidy up any areas that are still rough, give the whole thing a coat of finishing oil and you are done.

Higgledy-piggledy houses

THIS LAST PROJECT VARIES FROM THE REST IN THAT THERE IS NO DEFINITE END PRODUCT – YOU CAN DO WHATEVER YOU LIKE. THE REASON I HAVE INCLUDED IT IS THAT MANY CARVERS PREFER TO CARVE TO PATTERNS OR DESIGNS PROVIDED BY SOMEBODY ELSE.

This project develops as you go along and anything you can manage to include is perfectly acceptable. Many carvers I know who have attempted this make up their own stories to fit what they are carving, and a general theme develops as they go along. What I have carved is just an example of what you might like to do. You can follow it if you wish, or just use it to get you going and select bits of it for your design.

Mine is essentially a small house with a workshop above it and a garage and outhouse below, but don't be afraid to let your mind wander as far as you like to put something together.

TOOLBOX
- Knife and strop
- Safety glove
- Marker pen
- Small-bladed detail knife
- ⅛in (3mm) no. 3 palm gouge or similar
- ¼in (6mm) no. 3 palm gouge or similar
- ⅛in (3mm) no. 9 palm gouge if needed
- Finishing oil

Variations
You may like to apply a little colour to add a bit of character to your carving. Here are some examples that I have coloured, using acrylics diluted with about 20 parts water to 1 part paint.

1 The advantage of this project is that you can use any odd-shaped piece of wood from your workshop. The more random the shape, the better. My piece started out flat on one side, but this is not necessary.

2 Starting at the top, carve a pair of diagonals.

3 Carve to give the basic shape of the sides of a roof.

4 Add some vertical cuts to form the four walls of the building.

5 Don't be too fussy at this stage, as your ideas will develop as you go along.

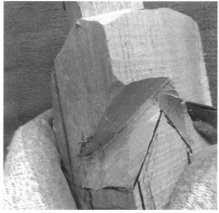

6 Draw your next house below the first, allowing a bit of space to accommodate the steps and so on.

7 Cut the angles of the roof on both sides as far back as you feel comfortable with.

8 Draw some thickness to the roof and cut back carefully, making sure that you don't break it off.

9 Set back the wall below the roof by about 1/16–1/8in (2–3mm).

10 Now you can start to mark out your first set of stairs, from the first building to the second. Be aware that you can only cut steps on a slope, so you will need to cut whatever slope you can fit on the available wood first.

11 Cut the stairs, adjusting as you go along to fit them into the space available. Turn them round onto a flat landing area below the house.

12 You can fill in the area between the houses with rocks, like this. Put in a line of windows to suggest internal stairs.

13 The spare wood you have beside the lower house **(A)** can be turned into steps and a fence **(B)**.

14 You will need to link the lower house with whatever you add below it, so add more steps.

15 As before, cut a slope first, then notch it to create individual steps.

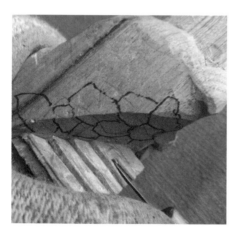

16 To form the tiles on the roofs, first cut a series of slopes from which the tiles can be cut.

17 Mark out the individual tiles and cut them with a small, sharp knife, taking care not to split the wood. Any minor blemishes can be made into broken tiles to add character.

18 When carving the doors and windows, show them slightly ajar: this makes them clearer and adds character.

19 Blank spaces can be filled with any detail you like to add. These archways are meant to suggest garages with vehicles in – I hope!

20 All that remains is to insert any small details that you feel would add to the carving. I usually give the whole thing a coat of oil to make for cleaner final cuts; butternut has a tendency to splinter a bit while carving. The whole piece can be oiled again when complete.

Suppliers

UK

KNIVES AND/OR GENERAL CARVING TOOLS

Ashley Iles (Edge Tools)
East Kirkby, Spilsby, Lincolnshire, PE23 4DD
www.ashleyiles.co.uk

Ben and Lois Orford
www.benandloisorford.com

Classic Hand Tools
Unit B, Hill Farm Business Park, Witnesham,
Ipswich, Suffolk IP6 9EW
www.classichandtools.com

Greenman Bushcraft
Unit 3/E, Beehive Business Centre, Beehive
Lane, Chelmsford, Essex, CM2 9TE
www.greenmanbushcraft.co.uk

Henry Taylor Tools
The Forge, Peacock Estate, Livesey Street,
Sheffield, S6 2BL
www.henrytaylortools.co.uk

Moonraker Knives
Rectory Cottage, West Knoyle, Warminster,
Wiltshire, BA12 6AF
www.moonrakerknives.co.uk

Nic Westermann (blades only)
Unit 7, Cemmaes Road, Machynlleth, Powys,
SY20 8LY
www.nicwestermann.co.uk

Toolnut
Unit 7, Beeching Close, Bexhill-on-Sea, East
Sussex, TN39 3YF
www.toolnut.co.uk

The Tool Post
Unit 7, Hawksworth, Southmead Industrial Park,
Didcot, Oxon, OX11 7HR
www.toolpost.co.uk

Workshop Heaven
Unit 5, The Spinney, Alkerton Oaks Business
Park, Stratford Road, Shenington, Banbury,
Oxon, OX15 6EP
www.workshopheaven.com

USA

KNIVES

Cape Forge
31 Berkshire Way, Simsbury, CT 06070
www.capeforge.com

Flexcut
8105 Hawthorne Drive, Erie, PA 16509
www.flexcut.com

Helvie Wood Carving Knives
PO Box 145, Tipton, IN 46072
www.helvieknives.com

Mastercarver
P O Box 5218, Grove City, FL 34224
www.mastercarver.com

R. Murphy Knives
13 Groton Harvard Road, Ayer, MA 01432
www.rmurphyknives.com

CARVING SUPPLIES

Stadtlander Woodcarvings
2951 Frost Road, Mantua, OH 44255
www.stadtlandercarvings.com

The Woodcraft Shop
2724 State Street, Bettendorf, IA 52722
www.thewoodcraftshop.com

AUSTRALIA & NEW ZEALAND

KNIVES AND/OR GENERAL CARVING TOOLS

Carbatec
128 Ingleston Road, Wakerley, QLD 4154 (and
see website for additional locations in Australia
and NZ) www.carbatec.com.au

Hobby Tools Australia
PO Box 20, Braeside, VIC 3195
www.hobbytools.com.au

Timbecon
Unit 2, Canvale Road, Canning Vale, WA 6155;
14 Roosevelt Street, Coburg North, VIC 3058
www.timbecon.com.au

About the author

Peter Benson started carving shortly after the end of World War II, on his return home to London after being an evacuee in the Suffolk countryside. Being a wartime child meant that much of what he wanted he had to make himself, hence his interest in making toys and models out of wood with a knife. Although in later years he graduated to more ambitious styles of carving, he still feels that much can be achieved with the minimum of tools. Peter spent his working life teaching physical education, finishing by running a special educational needs department. This period of his life convinced him that anyone can do anything with the right motivation and opportunity.

On his retirement in 1996, Peter set up the Essex School of Woodcarving, which is now based at his delightful thatched cottage in the north Essex countryside, where he lives with his wife Em and their dog Chance. Much of their time, when Peter is not writing for woodcarving journals, is spent travelling around teaching classes, holding workshops and judging competitions. Their travels have taken them to far-flung corners of the UK, Canada, Australia, France and 20 states of the USA.

Peter's personal passion in carving is centred on miniature work, especially the Japanese art of netsuke carving. He is the author of *The Art of Carving Netsuke* (GMC Publications, 2010). But this hasn't prevented him from being involved in several very large carvings, including a 2½-ton, life-sized polar bear, a memorial to the 49th West Riding Infantry Division, at the National Memorial Arboretum in Staffordshire, England.

Acknowledgements

Thanks to my wife Em for her patience and support while I was writing this book. Also to Em and my friend Dave Wilkins for helping with taking the photographs and putting up with my instructions

Thanks to Wendy McAngus and Stephen Haynes for their expertise in translating and correcting my submissions in order to put them into readable form. To my woodcarving friends worldwide for sharing their knowledge and techniques so willingly and to my American friends in particular for reinforcing the fact that carving really should be fun.

Index

A
abrasive paste 13
abrasives
  cellular 21, 37, 45
  grades of 29, 33, 37, 45, 111
adhesive, two-part epoxy 19
allergies to wood 14, 42
apple 14, 15, 22
apron 8, 11

B
ball-in-cage 112
bandsaw 34, 36, 50, 84
bark, removing 24, 26, 28, 41
basswood 14, 15, 34, 42, 58
birch 14, 34, 42, 46
blade 12, 18, 19
butternut 15, 96

C
coping saw 20, 36, 44, 50, 84
cuts, basic 16–17

D
drill 19, 20, 33
  bit, brad-pointed 33
drilling 38, 65, 84, 110, 115

F
face mask 14
fipple 40, 41
fruitwoods 14, 19, 34, 38,
  42, 46

G
glove, safety 8, 10, 11
gouge 8, 21, 33 36, 48, 61, 65,
  68, 70, 77, 86, 88, 95, 110, 116
green wood 8, 14, 15, 22, 25,
  50, 58

H
handle, making a custom 19
hardwood 14, 19, 102
hazel 14, 15, 30

J
jelutong 15, 58, 72

K
knife
  carrying in public 18
  choosing a 18–19
  fixed-blade 10, 18, 70
  folding 13, 18, 20
  sharpening a 12–13

L
lever cut 17
lime (linden) 14, 15, 34, 42,
  46, 58

M
maple 14, 34, 46

N
netsuke carving 127

O
oil, finishing 25, 29, 33, 37,
  41, 45, 49, 55, 81, 95, 117
oilstone 12

P
paint, acrylic 61, 65, 71, 77
pear 14
penknife 8, 9, 10
pith 26, 28, 29
pocketknife 8, 9, 10, 20
pull cut 17
push cut 16, 17, 24, 25

R
rabbet (rebate) plane 106
rasp 19
roughing out 20

S
safety glove 8, 10, 11
sanding 29, 33, 37, 48, 49,
  55, 71, 81, 95, 117
sap, bleeding 15, 42
sharpening plate, diamond 12
silver birch 15, 38, 42
spalting 14
spokeshave 19
squeeze cut 17
stop cut 16, 24, 26, 58, 64
strop 12, 13, 20
superglue 20, 70, 95, 101
sycamore 34, 38, 42, 46

T
template, card 109
thumb guard 17, 32
timber, non-toxic 42
toolbox 20–21

V
varnish 41, 65, 71, 77
vice, using a 38, 65

W
walnut 15, 19, 96
wedge cut 16, 24, 26, 64
wet and dry abrasive paper 12
wood 14, 15

Y
yew 19

To order a book, or to request a catalogue, contact: **GMC Publications Ltd**
Castle Place, 166 High Street, Lewes, East Sussex
BN7 1XU, United Kingdom
Tel: +44 (0)1273 488005
www.gmcbooks.com